TANKER BARGES ON THE HUMBER WATERWAYS

THE HUMBER WATERWAYS

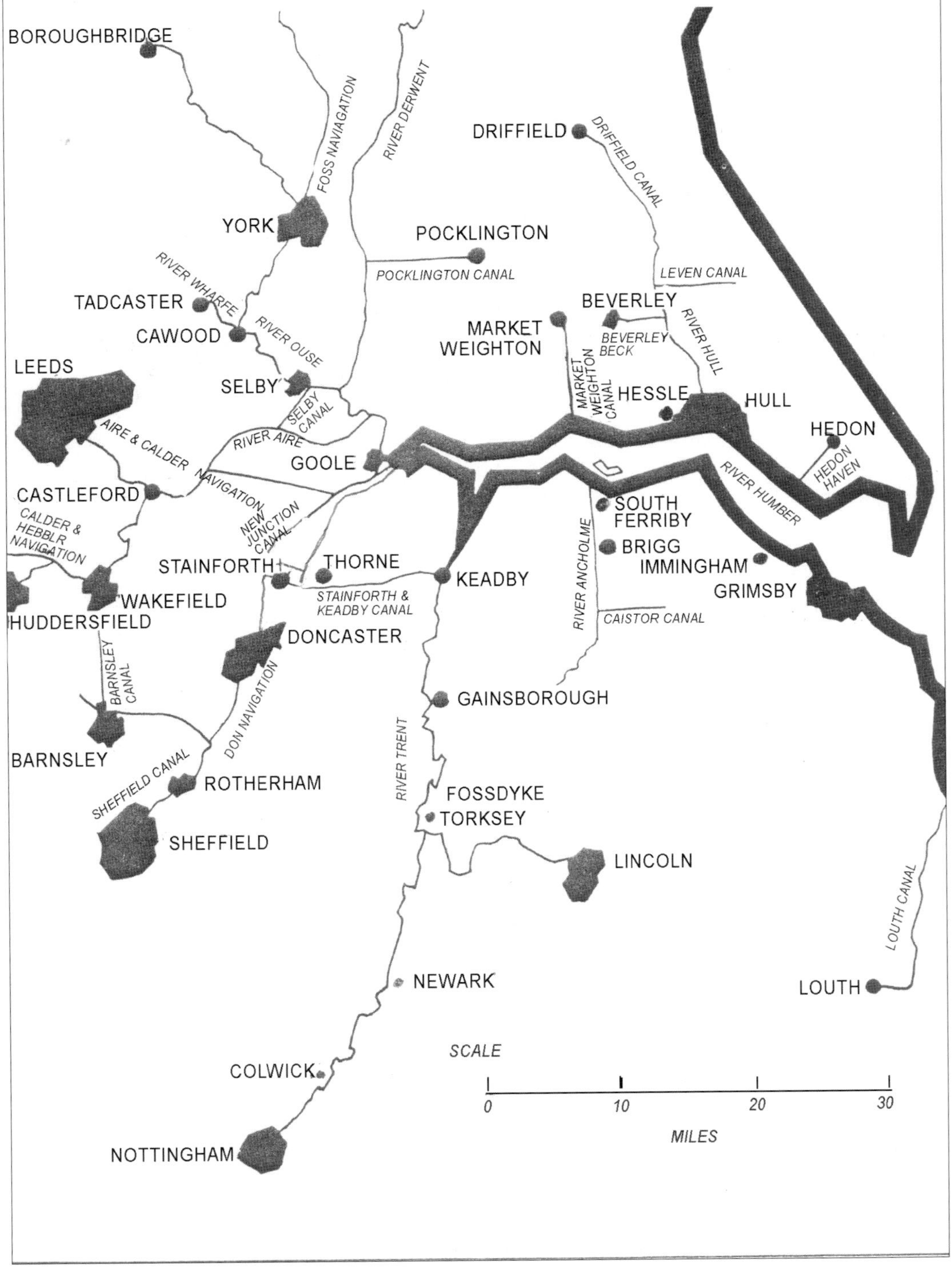

TANKER BARGES ON THE HUMBER WATERWAYS

MIKE TAYLOR

TEMPUS

Frontispiece: Map of the Humber Inland Waterways. (John Bryce)

First published 2006

Tempus Publishing Limited
The Mill, Brimscombe Port,
Stroud, Gloucestershire, GL5 2QG
www.tempus-publishing.com

British Library Cataloguing in Publication Data.
A catalogue record for this book is available from the British Library.

ISBN 0 7524 3921 9
978 0 7524 3921 1

Typesetting and origination by Tempus Publishing Limited.
Printed in Great Britain.

Contents

Acknowledgements

Maurice Bolton, Dave Hill, Bill Middleton, Arthur Potts, Albert Richards and Jarvis Whitton, as well as several now-deceased tanker crewmen, have provided much of the information used in this book. Numerous individuals, newspapers, companies and public bodies, credited in relevant captions, have kindly allowed me to use their photographs.

Books by Mike Taylor, published by Tempus:

The Calder and Hebble Navigation, 2002
The River Trent Navigation, 2000
The Sheffield and South Yorkshire Navigation, 2001
Shipping on the Humber (North Bank), 2003
Shipping on the Humber (South Bank), 2003
The Yorkshire Ouse Navigation, 2002
Tugs and Towing Barges on the Humber Waterways, 2006

Harkers' *Fusedale H* entering Bulholme Lock on the Aire & Calder Network, bound for Leeds.

Introduction

Barrels of fresh water for ships in the Humber were carried by barge from the earliest days of the ports. By the late nineteenth century, vegetable oils from Hull's seed crushing industry, carboys of sundry chemicals and some of the products of coal distillation had been added to this traffic in liquids on local waterways.

In the early twentieth century, the drums and other containers in which these various liquids were carried aboard wooden barges and lighters began to be phased out with the construction of barges having iron tanks within them ('double-skin ships'), enabling much heavier cargoes to be carried. These were built primarily to carry liquid coal tar from coke ovens to tar distilleries and collect creosote, one of the products.

John Harker of Knottingley and John H. Whitaker of Hull were both active in this field and both men subsequently gave their names to companies which later specialised in the carriage of petrol. In the late nineteenth century, paraffin for lamps was almost the only crude oil product to be of commercial use. The demand for petrol began about 1900 and 'Pratt's Motor Spirit' was supplied by the Anglo-American Oil Company in green 2-gallon cans, sold by ironmongers, post offices and even chemists until the 1920s when the more familiar garage pumps were gradually introduced. These were supplied with petrol delivered in bulk from local storage depots that were often fed by tanker barge. From then on, demand for petrol started to reach unprecedented levels year after year, as the motor car continued its rise in popularity and petrol effectively catalysed development of the tanker barge.

At first, petrol was carried in double-skin ships similar to those used for coal tar cargoes, but by 1920 these were steadily being replaced by purpose-built iron or steel tanker barges. Dumb craft such as Whitakers' *Coalite* and Majors' three lighters were amongst the first of these tankers in the region and were followed some years later by powered barges such as Anglo-American Oil's *Tetney* and Harkers' *Michael*. Until the double-skinned *Rix Merlin*, launched in 2005, almost all subsequent tankers were 'single skin ships' where the liquid cargo was separated from the water in which it was carried by only the thin steel plates of a vessel's hull. Transverse and longitudinal partitions – which subdivided the cargo space into several separate tanks – prevented surging of the liquid and consequent instability when the vessel was under way.

By the early 1950s, all new tanker barges were self-propelled and almost all dumb barges had been motorised, a practice begun in the 1930s. Tanker barges on the Humber then reached a peak in both numbers and total tonnage capacity in the late 1950s and early 1960s, before a gradual decline in number of craft, as bigger vessels were built. There was also a falling off in demand for waterborne deliveries due to competition from long-distance pipelines and the financial advantages of deliveries by road and rail, effectively given by successive governments.

In the Humber region, tanker traffic flourished on the more industrial waterways such as the Aire & Calder Navigation (A&CN), the Sheffield & South Yorkshire Navigation (S&SYN),

The Coal Tar Industry

During the first half of the twentieth century, coal was strongly heated in a furnace to produce 'town gas' for domestic and industrial users. These 'gasworks' were situated in almost every town in the country and, in addition to producing coal gas, the coal gave off a vapour which condensed to two immiscible liquids, ammoniacal liquor and coal tar. A solid residue of coke remained. The two liquids obtained were usually trasnported to tar works, often by barge, where ammonia, to manufacture fertilisers, was liberated from the liquor by chemical treatment and the tar was fractionally distilled, as described in the table opposite. The creosote produced was often then carried away by tanker barge; the pitch by dry cargo vessel.

Condensation Range	Name of Fraction	Uses
200'C-250'C	chemical oil	various chemicals are removed from the oil and what remains is added to the creosote
250'C-350'C	creosote	wood preservation
Residue	pitch	separated into different grades of hardness and used for waterproofing, roadmaking and electrode manufacture.

Hull's Old Harbour and the rivers Ancholme, Ouse and Trent. Tanker traffic rarely, if ever, frequented the smaller and more rural Humber waterways, such as the Louth Canal, Market Weighton Canal, The Calder & Hebble Navigation above Wakefield, the Fossdyke and the rivers Derwent and Hull above Hull.

Illustrations have been arranged in a rough chronological order to give a feel for the historical development of craft. Sizes of craft are occasionally quoted in captions and here references to 'Trent size' (82½ft x 14½ft) and 'Sheffield size' (61½ft x 15½ft) will be met. Cargo capacity is perhaps more meaningful than dimensions and this has increased over the years from less than 100 tons to nearly 700 tons. Even this is not truly representative of the amount of liquid carried because neap tides and low summer river levels have always permitted passage of only partially loaded tankers, especially in the upper reaches of tidal rivers. This has always been of major significance for vessels passing through Naburn lock bound up the Ouse for York and Cromwell lock when heading up the Trent to Newark or Nottingham.

Perhaps surprisingly, little fuel oil was carried, apart from that for bunkering purposes, until after the Second World War when a greater number of uses for it were found and tankers with heating coils to keep the normally viscous liquid mobile were developed in the 1950s, mainly by Harkers. Another change, happening at about the same time and continuing to this day, was the lengthening of craft, enabling them to carry greater payloads.

Initially, tanker barges usually loaded at Saltend, on the north bank of the Humber, but also at Killingholme on the opposite bank. Ship-fed storage tanks were sited at these locations and also at Keadby and Hook, near Goole. Petroleum fractions were delivered here from refineries elsewhere in Britain and Europe. In 1969, however, the Associated Petroleum Terminal, jointly

The Petroleum Industry

Crude oil (petroleum) is a mixture of many chemicals having different boiling points. When it is heated in an oil refinery, most of it is vapourised, leaving a residue of bitumen. The vapour produced is passed into the base of a fractioning column, usually over 100ft tall, which has a temperature of about 400°C at its base, falling to less than 20°C at its top. The vapours pass up the column and all except the petroleum gases condense (turn to liquid) at different boiling points. The various liquids produced are then run off into separate tanks for storage and the crude oil is thus split into several fractions, detailed in the table below, and ready for distribution by road, rail or water. LPG (liquified petroleum gases) are carried by tanker barges on the waterways of mainland Europe but not in the UK. All other fractions, apart from bitumen, have been common cargoes on the Humber waterways.

By the late 1910s there were storage tanks for petroleum products delivered by ship at Saltend, near Hull, but the Humber had no refineries of its own until the Lindsey Refinery (opened in 1968) and Humber Refinery (opened in 1969) were built on its south bank at Killingholme, near Immingham.

Condensation Range	Name of Fraction		Uses
above 20'c	petroleum gases		LPG fuel and Calor Gas for small stoves
20'C-180'C	petrol	Collectively known as clean oils, light oils, white oils or white spirit	motor car fuel
160'C-250'C	kerosene		jet aircraft fuel paraffin for heating
220'C-350'C	light gas oil		diesel engine fuel
320'C-400'C	fuel oil	Collectively known as black oils	fuel for ships, power stations and other furnaces
	heavy gas oil		lubricating oil for machinery
residue	bitumen		roofing and road surfacing

owned by the petroleum companies Fina, Total and Conoco, was opened at Immingham on the south bank, linked to two new large oil refineries which processed the crude oil delivered by large ocean-going tankers and fed products back to the barge berths on the jetty. Thus, the Humber acquired its own petroleum fractionating facilities and almost all barge loading was then transferred to here, though black oil continued to be collected from Saltend for a few more years.

Separate chapters are devoted to the boatyards where many of these tanker barges were built and to the interconversions of dry cargo craft to tanker barges and vice versa.

There are a few instances of the duplication of pictures used in my other Tempus books, listed above, where only one picture of a particular vessel seems to exist. Each photograph is credited separately, apart from those taken by me or selected from my collection, which are uncredited. I have also interspersed amongst the illustrations some recollections of men who worked on or with tankers.

Note:

(a) It may be worthwhile to reiterate the generally accepted definitions of barges (flat-bottomed freight boats) and lighters (barges used for transporting goods, especially in loading and unloading ships), and also to state that 'dumb' refers to a vessel not having an engine.

(b) I have seen published works where 'tonnes' is regarded as an alternative spelling of 'tons'. Actually 1 ton = 1.016 tonnes, and there was a general changeover to the metric 'tonnes' late in the twentieth century. However, since the capacities of craft quoted in this book are only approximate, I have regarded the two units to be identical and quoted 'tons'. Another change, happening at about the same time and also linked to our membership of the European Community, has been the replacement of 'inflammable' by 'flammable' in the labelling of certain cargoes.

Mike Taylor, 2006

one

To the end of the 1920s

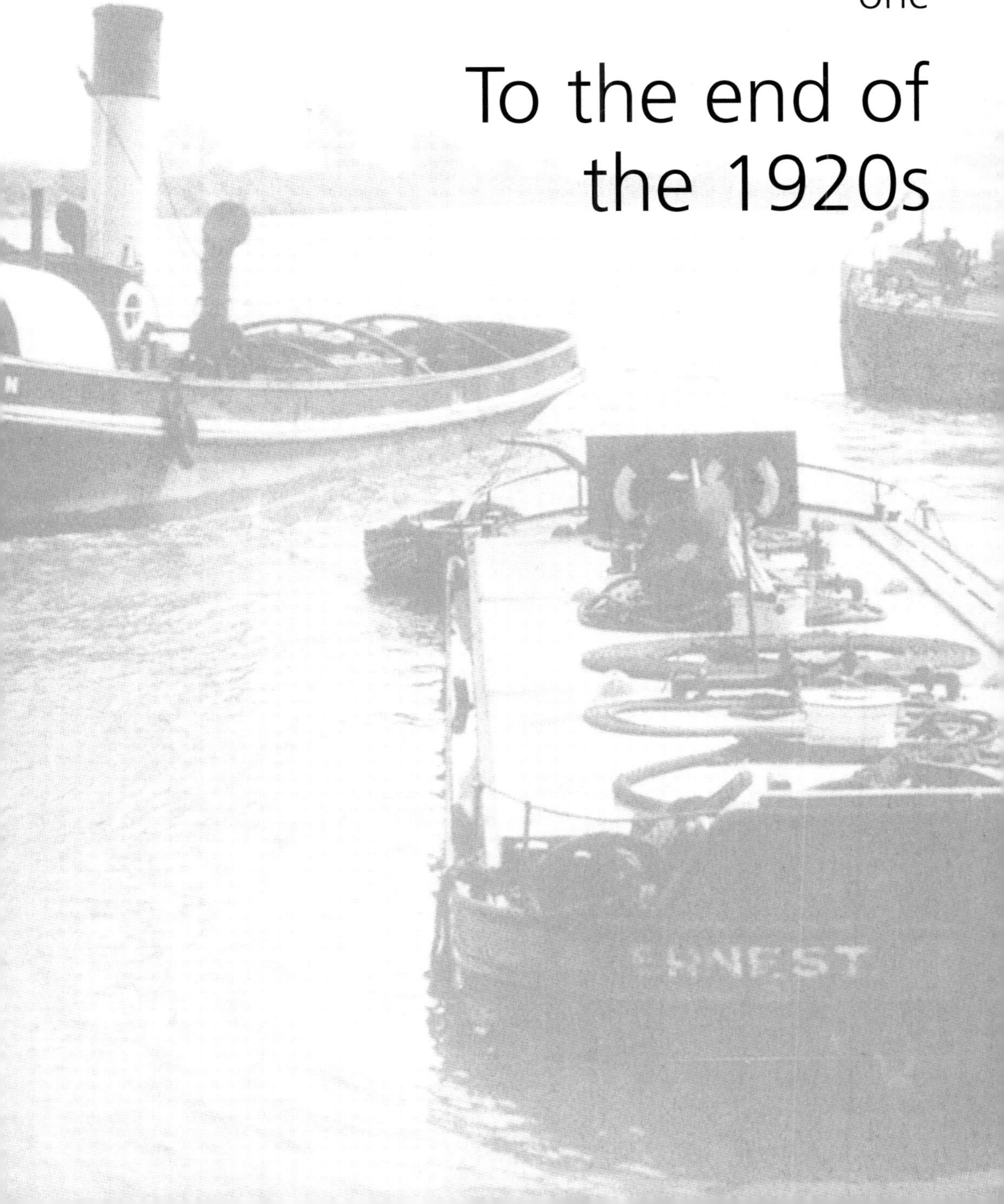

Richard Dunston of Thorne, Henry Scarr of Hessle and the Yorkshire Dry Dock Co. (YDDC) of Hull were major builders of early iron/steel inland waterway tanker craft in the region. A few craft were built by Watsons of Gainsborough and Cook, Welton & Gemmell at Beverley.

Harkers' and Whitakers' fleets were augmented by vessels built by the oil companies Anglo-American Oil (later Esso) and Russian Oil Products in the earliest carriage of petrol on the Humber waterways. Harkers, however, rapidly became the dominant carrier and by 1929–30 were delivering nearly 100,000 tons of petroleum products annually, of which 75,500 tons were petrol.

During the 1920s and throughout the 1930s, most of these cargoes were collected from storage tanks at Saltend, near Hull, where the first jetty was constructed in 1914, though a few came from Keadby on the river Trent. Initially the tanks were fed by coasters from refineries on the Tees.

By the end of the 1920s, deliveries of petrol by barge were being made to Anglo-American's premises at Brigg, Castleford, Leeds and York, Majors' depot at Hunslet, Medway Oil & Storage's Nottingham and Wakefield depots, National Benzole Company's depots at Hunslet and Sheffield, Russian Oil Products' premises at Rotherham, Sealand's depot at Hunslet, and Shell's tanks at Hunslet and Wakefield.

Harkers' *Harry*, *George* and *Edward* moored in Goole docks after delivering barrels of creosote to ships from the Aire Tar Works at Knottingley early in the twentieth century.

Harkers' tank barge *John Tom* on the inside, and beyond, coal barge *Tom*, probably bound for York via Bank Dole lock, tied up outside Aire Tar Works at Knottingley. Harkers' business began with carriage of tar collected by barge from gasworks at Monckton on the Barnsley Canal, Stourton, on the A&CN near Leeds, and York. It was delivered here for refinement before final products were exported via Goole.

The wooden 88½ft x 17½ft *Majors' No 2*, one of the three earliest purpose-built tanker lighters, nearing completion in 1907 for Majors, the coal tar distillers, at Geo. Cooper's Garrison side yard, off the river Hull. The dry dock is now the site of a car park outside Whitakers' offices.

Above: The three Majors' lighters (*No 1, No 2* and *No 3*) were purchased by Whitakers in 1922–23 and became *Yorkist 1, Yorkist 2* and *Yorkist 3* respectively. Whitakers' steam tug *Ackworth* is seen in King George Dock entrance lock with the lighter *Yorkist 3*, in 1951.

The 61½ft x 15½ft (Sheffield size) dumb tanker *Coalite* was purchased by Whitakers in 1910, shortly after its completion by Joseph Scarr at Beverley. It had a capacity of 100 tons and was used for carrying coal tar and coal tar products on local rivers and canals. On occasions, *Coalite* carried gas oil, a petroleum fraction that could be used to supplement coal gas supplies for domestic and industrial use, to York gasworks. The vessel was horse-hauled on canals and sailed on rivers until an engine was installed in 1931. It is shown here in Hull Docks. (Whitakers)

Opposite below: Cook, Welton & Gemmell built the 60ft x 15ft steam tanker lighter *Tetney* in 1909 for the Tetney Oil & Manure Co. of Grimsby who sold it in 1917 to Anglo-American Oil. It was then used for several years to deliver paraffin from Hull to York. The tanker is shown here in Grimsby Docks.

Left: Coalite as it would appear as a sailing keel. The illustration is taken from a montage of Whitaker craft, prepared to commemorate a retirement of one of the Whitakers in the 1990s. (Whitakers)

Below: Non-petroleum liquids were being carried on the Humber waterways throughout most of the twentieth century and the 73ft x 20ft, 180-ton capacity dumb lighter *Tit*, built by Cochranes of Selby in 1925 for John H. Scott of Hull is shown having its cargo of edible oil pumped off by the factory's steam pumps at a wharf on the river Hull. (Whitakers)

In 1925, Anglo-American Oil had the steel motor tanker *Fossgate* (right) and dumb tanker *Lowgate* built by Scarrs at Hessle. They are seen in snow at their builders' yard. Both craft were 58½ft x 14½ft, had capacities of 60 tons and 70 tons respectively, and were designed to work as a motor-dumb pair to their owners' York depot.

Anglo-American Oil had the 97ft x 17ft coaster *Caldergate* built at Amble on the east coast, north of Tynemouth. Seen here at sea, the vessel, registered at Hull, made several voyages to its owners' depots at Castleford and Leeds Dock.

STORAGE TANKS of any Description, any SHAPE, any SIZE, either RIVETED or WELDED BY EXPERTS.

ONE OF MANY PETROL STORAGE TANKS WE HAVE MADE FOR BARGES.

Our Works practically adjoin the SUSPENSION BRIDGE, South Accommodation Rd, LEEDS

Harkers purchased the Sheffield size wooden keel *Two Sisters* in 1922 and had three tanks and a new deck fitted by Dunstons. The tanks are all too evident in this 1926 photograph of the remains of the vessel after an explosion at Keadby whilst loading petrol for Sheffield in 1926. The accident, caused by a faulty valve which had been fitted with an improvised adjustment, killed the captain and his young mate.

Right: After the *Two Sisters* explosion, Harkers dispensed with wooden vessels and had several motor and dumb barges built by Dunstons. The dumb Sheffield size tanker barge *Marjory* lies ready for launching in 1927. *Ada, Charlotte, Denise, Dorothy, Ernest, Jim, Marjory* and *Ruth* were all dumb Sheffield size 100-ton capacity iron boats with tanks dropped in, built by Dunstons.

Opposite above: Harkers had the Sheffield size motor towing barge *Michael* built by Dunstons in 1925 and it is shown here undergoing trials at Thorne. This was to be the only self-propelled vessel in the company's fleet for the next couple of years. It had a capacity of 80 tons but carried only 75 tons when working to Sheffield.

Opposite below: Until the late 1920s, most liquids were carried in unpowered wooden craft with iron tanks fitted. This advertisement for the supply and fitting of such tanks was published by the Oxley Engineering Co. of Leeds.

Harkers' Sheffield size, 100-ton capacity, dumb purpose-built tanker barge *Jim*, launched by Dunstons in 1927, arriving at Keadby to load petrol for Sheffield.

George Beckett, Boatman

Skippers on the Sheffield run in the 1920s all lived at Thorne and we based our barges there. I had *Jim*, I owned a horse and was expected to find a mate/horse handler for the trips.

On day one, we went down to Keadby, loaded and came back to Thorne. Next day, we hoped to get as far as Mexborough or Swinton so that we could reach Lumley Street depot at Sheffield, be pumped off and get part-way back on the third day, leaving us to get back to Thorne on day four. This was the only day when we worked less than twelve hours. Harkers expected us to do three trips a fortnight. Regular deliveries were essential and, if the river was in flood, they paid for us to hire extra horses at Doncaster.

After *Two Sisters* exploded at Keadby, we had to take some ridiculous safety precautions. These didn't prevent another wooden keel with iron tanks dropped in, owned by Whitakers, from exploding on the Aire & Calder at New Bridge in 1929. No heating and no flames were allowed aboard. Matches had to be kept under lock and key and we even had to light navigation lights off the boat. We couldn't live aboard and used to sleep in lock lobbies in winter or in the open air on deck on fine summer nights, lying on sacks and covering ourselves with horse blankets. The horse got a better deal in the stables than we did. We only had the cold food we'd brought with us and relied on lockkeepers to put the kettle on when we telephoned ahead.

The nearest I came to an accident was when a cyclist threw a lighted match into the canal at Thorne after I had been doing some tank cleaning. Huge flames shot up from the canal and raced towards us. I stopped them just short of *Jim* by using the fire extinguisher.

Harkers' *Ernest*, another Sheffield size, 100-ton capacity, Dunston-built (in 1927) dumb tanker, waiting in the river Trent outside the S&SYN entrance lock at Keadby, having loaded petrol for Sheffield at Saltend and been towed upriver by United Towing Co.'s steam tug *Krooman*. Towage by horse to its destination would probably take place after the tanker had penned up into the canal.

Harkers' *Sabina H* first brought petrol to Brigg from Saltend as a dumb barge, when new, in 1929. It is shown leaving South Ferriby lock to join the Ancholme Navigation, on another voyage to Brigg in 1950, by which time the tanker had delivered hundreds of cargoes to this Lincolnshire storage depot and been motorised, with its capacity cut from 100 tons to 75 tons.

A dumb tanker that had been towed up from Saltend moored on the river Aire above Knostrop flood lock using the Hunslet depot's pumps to discharge its cargo of petrol.

The Sealand Petroleum Co. established a petrol depot at Hunslet and had the Trent size (82½ft x 14½ft), 90-ton capacity, motor tanker barge *Sealand* built in 1929 by Watsons of Gainsborough. The vessel is shown discharging petrol at the depot in that same year.

two

The 1930s and 1940s

Harkers purchased two disused boatyards standing on land adjacent to Skew Bridge at Knottingley in 1929 and began building their own craft there after attracting several of Dunstons' workforce away from Thorne.

During a twenty-eight-year period when they built no new craft, YDDC produced Whitakers' first motor barge by installing an engine in *Vincit*, whilst Anglo-American continued operating their craft as in the 1920s. These were joined in delivering petrol in the 1930s by James W. Cook & Co. and the Medway Oil & Storage Co. This was at a time when motor barges, usually powered by diesel engines of between 100 and 120hp, were replacing dumb craft and the petrol carriers also followed this trend. Cooks began operating on the Humber in 1930, having bought out Sealand and renamed the tanker *Sealand* (see page 22) *Seamew C*. They had several new 'skin ships' built at both Thorne and Hessle, Dunstons having taken over Scarrs of Hessle in 1931. Medway Oil & Storage began in the mid-1930s with several tankers built in the late 1920s at Alblasserdam in the Netherlands, renamed in their style. Then they had new craft built in the mid-1930s, again at Thorne and Hessle. After the Second World War, Harkers introduced bunkering tankers with heated tanks to fuel the increasing numbers of oil-fired ships visiting the Humber ports.

The craft in operation were steadily becoming more sophisticated during this period. Aladdin stoves which could burn safely in an atmosphere of petrol vapour, were installed, allowing crews to live aboard their vessels. New craft were fitted with their own pumps for discharging cargoes, and a few bunkering tankers were provided with VHF radio for contact with their shore-based offices. Radar, developed during the Second World War, was not yet available and captains had the discretion over whether a tanker moved or not in fog.

Collection of cargoes was still mainly from Saltend, whilst a major water-served depot at Colwick, below Nottingham, was opened between 1930 and 1933, by several petrol companies acting jointly. Cargoes were usually brought here by motor-dumb tanker pairs, this being a convenient means of coping with the 82½ft x 14½ft (Trent size) bottleneck created by Newark Town lock. Sixty tankers, including twenty powered craft, were working on the Trent by 1939. Other smaller petrol depots were opened on the Trent at Newark and Farndon Field, above the town, as well as at Hexthorpe on the S&SYN, and at Hook, above Goole, on the Ouse. This latter depot was designed to be serviced by coastal tanker, but received barge deliveries on neap tides when the sea-going vessels found difficulty of access.

The 120ft x 17ft coastal tanker *Constance H* nearing completion at the former Garlick part of Harkers' yard in 1930. The tanker was powered by a 150hp Widdop diesel engine. As well as trading around the British coast, it delivered many cargoes of creosote from the A&CN to Teesside in the 1930s.

Syd Woods, Skipper of *Constance H*

Before a refinery was built on Humberside, petrol was shipped to Saltend and Keadby from Teesside. A Leeds dealer later decided to get his from the Thames and, for a couple of years, *Constance H* used to collect it from Coryton and bring it all the way up the east coast, into the Humber and along the Aire and Calder Navigation. It also did occasional trips from Coryton to Exeter and even Rotterdam with white spirit.

I took over in 1935 after heating coils had been fitted and the original Widdop engine replaced by a 220hp Crossley. We sometimes worked to near-European ports, but mainly, collected about 130 tons of creosote from Yorkshire Tar Distillers at Stourton, near Leeds, or Knottingley and delivered it to ICI's Billingham wharf on the river Tees. This trip had everything; canal, river and sea and, during one three-month spell in 1937, we made twenty-nine return voyages between the Aire & Calder and the Tees. We were often the only vessel to head out to sea past Spurn in bad weather leaving the larger ships sheltering in the Humber. The six-man crew were busiest on the canal though. We were on the bottom for much of the time and, to get under the bridges, even with the wheelhouse down, we had to carry as much water up as creosote we brought back.

I left the ship in 1938 before it went for war service at Scapa Flow, with a gun fitted. After the war it traded from Hull to King's Lynn for a while and regularly from Leeds to Rouen before being sold in 1948 as a bunkering barge.

Harkers' 75-ton capacity steam tanker barge *Lincoln*, with its off-set funnel, was built in 1903 by Watsons of Gainsborough and converted to a tanker by Harkers after purchase by them in the 1930s. The vessel was then used to bring tar from York gasworks to the tar works shown, on Bank Dole cut at Knottingley, then owned by Yorkshire Tar Distillers. It replaced the wooden craft *George* and *John Tom* on this traffic which lasted until the 1950s, by which time it had been converted to diesel power. During the Second World War, *Lincoln* worked between York and Knottingley, loaded in both directions; a rarity for a tanker barge. Tar was brought away from York as before, but a blended mixture of pitch and creosote was carried up to the city's glassworks to be used as a substitute for fuel oil in its furnaces. (Alan Faulkner Collection)

Opposite above: In the 1930s, Shell established a petrol depot in Barnsley and one of Harkers' horse-drawn tankers is seen discharging a cargo there in the mid-1930s with Mill Street bridge in the background.

Opposite below: Harkers' 1934-built, 100-ton capacity, Trent size motor tanker *Carson* lying loaded at Shell's wooden jetty inside Hedon Haven, near Saltend. The vessel was fitted with a 145hp Petter engine.

INFLAMMABLE
INFLAMMABLE

George Martin, Harkerman

I began with Harkers as a horse marine in 1932 and eventually drifted into working full-time on their tankers.

My first trip to Nottingham was on *Charlotte.* We were at the back of *Ted* being towed by *Vinny. Charlotte* was the clumsiest boat I've ever known. We shoved and pulled at that tiller 'til our backs were red raw and our arms were six feet long. It used to be two hours on and two hours off steering on an open deck in all weathers. In bad weather, I used to wear an overcoat with oilskins on top. You daren't let your clothing get wet because there was no heating aboard to dry it out.

Friction was a problem with those big barges when you came out of a lock. They were skin ships and there's a concrete wall maybe a 150 yards long at the top side of those Trent locks. If the ship got alongside it, you couldn't get her off and she'd trail along the wall with sparks flying so you had to try to get her stern off by putting the helm hard over. With luck, she'd then just rub with her bow where that wooden bumper was. It was sparks near the cargo that set fire to *Bertha* after she'd rubbed against Town Bridge at Gainsborough in 1934. That happened because she was a skin-ship.

I became captain of *Michael* on the Sheffield run, towing *Jim* or *Ernest* in 1938. It was then a three-day round trip rather than the four-day job it had been with horse boats.

Harkers' 100-ton capacity 150hp Trent size towing barge *Victor H* towing a dumb barge up the Humber at Walker Dykes on its maiden voyage in 1936. Both vessels would be bound for the Trent, loaded with petrol for Colwick and would have left Saltend at the 'first of flood' to get maximum assistance from the incoming tide.

Whitakers' steam towing barge *Gainsborough* (right) and two of the company's dumb barges *T.P. Bullard* and *Whitakers No.5* are tied up at Goole whilst returning to either Goole or Selby after delivering oil to Watsons' soap works at Leeds.

Concentrating at the time mainly on tug-towed dumb dry cargo craft, Whitakers tanker traffic took second place in their activities, though they carried petrol and oils in their tanker barges. A 100hp Gardner diesel engine and tanks were fitted into their dumb barge *Vincit* in 1937, making it the company's first motor barge, here coming up the river Hull loaded. *Vincit* was built by Henry Scarr at Hessle in 1915 as a water boat and converted by YDDC to carry 230 tons of fuel oil. (Whitakers)

George Chester, Boatman with Whitakers 1935–1975

That direct engine they fitted on *Vincit* had to be stopped before it would run in reverse and this caused all sorts of problems, including the need for a lot of 'lucky lassoing' whenever we were in a tight spot. I was mate on it before the war running petrol day-in-day-out from Saltend to Majors at Leeds. It was converted to a black-oiler during the war and had a coal stove fitted into its fore cabin.

In 1941 I moved as captain to Whitakers' motorised lighter *No.45*. This was 61ft x 15ft and just able, after its rubbing strakes had been chopped off, to pass through river lock into the river Aire and up to Watsons' soap works. We brought lots of palm oil here from Selby mills or from ships in King George or Alex Docks at Hull. Usually there were at least two tanker lighters loaded besides *No.45*. *No.45* carried 60 tons and the lighters loaded about 240 tons between them. They were brought up to Leeds by one of Whitakers' steam tugs and I came up under my own feeble power, with great difficulty sometimes on that 'five-mile pond' between Ferrybridge and Castleford. At Leeds, we all went into the Tatie Basin and, over the next couple of days, I made about six trips to Watsons and back to discharge the cargo because I was the only one who could get there. The steam tug powered the pumps on the lighters to pump their cargoes into *No.45* in the Tatie Basin and I was discharged at Watsons by their shore-based pumps.

I was made captain of *Jondor* when it was new in 1950 and for four years it carried 250 tons of petrol from Saltend to Leeds, at least twice a week. Then they fitted heating coils and a boiler to it and for the next twenty years I had it on the York glassworks run with the occasional bunkering job in Grimsby fish docks. We shared the glassworks deliveries with Harkers and *Jondor* had to carry up 230 tons each week. For most of the year this involved one trip a week but in summer, when low river levels coincided with neap tides, problems with sand bars below Naburn locks meant that 70 tons was the maximum cargo and three round trips became necessary each week. Selby bridges were also a problem on the York run. I used to come through them stern-first on big tides for safety. They used to swing both rail and road bridges at the same time but once when I was running the bridges, I saw the rail bridge opening and assumed that the toll bridge, around a slight bend, had opened, but found I was wrong. It was shut against me and flattened my wheelhouse as I went under it.

After I had retired, I was persuaded to come back for a year on Whitakers' diesel tug *Cawood*. One of the jobs we did was when Fishpond lock was being rebuilt. The tankers coming to Leeds pumped their loads into one above the lock which made the delivery and we pulled the one below the lock back down the canal in reverse for a couple of miles through Woodlesford lock until it could turn at Fleet.

Opposite above: The 93ft x 21½ft *Linklight* was built by Watsons as a 'sailing tank barge' for a London company in 1927. Fitted with two auxiliary Kromhout diesel engines, the vessel sank in Margate Sound before making its maiden voyage and, after being raised, was brought back to Gainsborough. Whitakers eventually purchased the vessel in 1947 and installed a Lister engine before using it for bunkering purposes. The vessel is shown outside Whitakers' Crown Dry Dock site in Hull Harbour.

Opposite below: Anglo-American Oil's *Caldergate* and *Lowgate* loading at Anglo-American jetty, half a mile above the Shell jetty in Hedon Haven, near Saltend, in the late 1930s. (Jarvis Whitton)

JOHN.H.WHITAKER. LD

Left: Two of James W. Cook & Co.'s early Trent size Thorne-built tankers, *Drake C* (left) and *Dauntless C*, both launched in 1930, lightly loaded along with other craft below Newark Nether lock, bound further up the Trent for Colwick. (Les Reid)

Below: Cooks' 100-ton capacity motor tanker *Shearwater C*, Hessle-built in 1935, heads up the Trent between Torksey and Newark, bound for Colwick, with one of the company's dumb craft in tow.

Above: Cooks' 130-ton capacity motor tanker barge *Snipe C*, built by Dunstons in 1940, on acceptance trials in the Humber.

Below: A lightly loaded Cooks' motor-dumb tanker barge tow heading up the Trent encounters one of the hazards of that navigation as it approaches craft grounded by lack of water blocking the channel near Meering ferry close to Besthorpe. Bill Middleton suggested that the towing barge could be either *Curlew C* or *Cormorant* C.

Medway Oil's 79ft x 14ft, 120-ton capacity dumb tanker *Veracitie* was built in 1929 in Holland and re-registered at Hull in 1936. It is shown here, slightly obscured, above Newark Town lock in the late 1930s whilst waiting to head further upriver.

Medway Oil's 1929-built former Dutch tanker *Fidelitie*, after lengthening in 1938 to become 105ft x 17½ft, 120-ton capacity, heading up the Humber in the mid-1940s.

Above: Medway Oil's Sheffield size 80-ton capacity Dunston-built *Mobilitie* on Humber trials in 1938. The tanker worked to Rotherham depot both before and after the Second World War.

Right: The small 135-ton capacity tanker barge *Equality*, built in 1938 at Beverley by Cook, Welton & Gemmell for the Hull Trawler Supply Co. delivering water to trawlers in Hull's St Andrew's Dock.

Yorkshire Tar Distillers' 60-ton capacity, horse-drawn tanker barge *Alice* tied up outside Manvers Main colliery on the Dearne & Dove Canal as its crew heads for the works canteen. The vessel has come to collect tar for delivery to its owners' plant at Kilnhurst.

Harkers built the 70-ton capacity, Sheffield size *Daphne H* at Knottingley in 1936 and, together with *Michael H* (see page 18) it took over petrol deliveries to Sheffield from the horse-drawn tankers. After the Second World War, *Daphne* was fitted with pre-fabricated crew accommodation and this is evident as the vessel passes Hexthorpe whilst returning to Saltend for reloading, the former storage tanks at Keadby having now become disused.

Above: A petrol depot was built at Hexthorpe, near Doncaster, on the S&SYN in the late 1930s and the crews of *Vinny H* (Knottingley-built in 1935 with a capacity of 100 tons and a 125hp Crossley diesel engine) and *John George H* (Knottingley-built in 1932 with a capacity of 110 tons and a 100hp Widdop engine) pass the time of day as the latter vessel is being discharged there.

Right: Harkers' dumb tanker *Marjory H* (see page 19) stuck along with *Dorothy H* on the frozen river Ouse, below Goole, in early 1947. The craft, bound for Leeds, were being towed upriver by Harkers' tug *Lion*. *Marjory* worked overseas during the Second World War and was found at Ghent in 1944. After repair, the vessel was returned to the Humber in 1946.

In early 1947, several of the smaller Harker tankers were taken out into the river Aire at Knottingley and laid up. Bank Dole lock house, part of *Ernest H* and the almost submerged bottom gates of the lock are shown a couple of months later after severe spring flooding. (Jarvis Whitton)

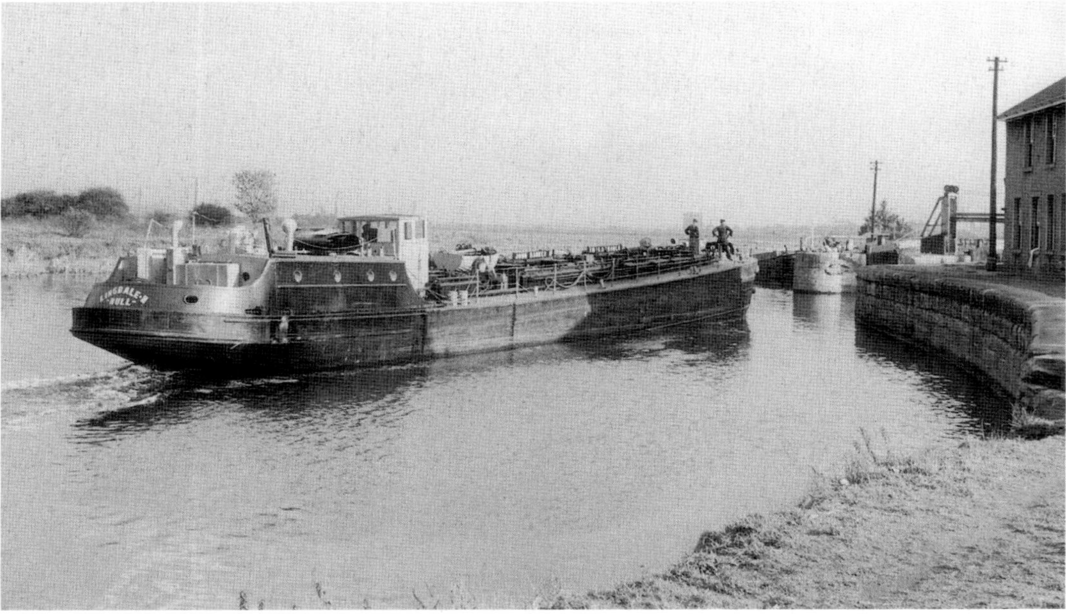

Harkers' 124ft x 17½ft 240-ton capacity, 1948-built *Lingdale H*, fitted with a 120hp Blackstone main engine, approaches Ferrybridge flood lock whilst coming light down the A&CN.

three

The 1950s

Having had earlier tankers built for their Humber work at Thorne and Hessle, Cooks set up their own yard at Wivenhoe in Essex after the Second World War and began building them there until it was taken over by Corys in 1958.

At Knottingley, Harkers extended their premises in 1950 by opening Point End slipway, across the canal from their yard. This was modified and reconstructed in 1954 enabling it to accommodate three 140ft-long tankers side by side for inspection, repair or maintenance. They also motorised the remaining dumb tankers in their fleet and built thirty-nine new tankers for themselves during the decade, fitting them with engines of around 150hp. The yard was so busy that Cook, Welton & Gemmell (CWG) built six vessels for them at Beverley in 1952–53. Much of this activity was due to removal, in 1952, of the bottleneck at Newark which had hitherto restricted tankers passing through Town Lock to Trent size. Harkers could then take larger and more economic loads to Colwick and reached their peak of activity on the Humber waterways. They had forty-five motor tankers operating there in 1957, but then gradually withdrew their smaller vessels. Whitakers began the decade by having three motor tankers built at Dunstons, but they then had their own YDDC subsidiary construct three more a few years later. In 1954, Jet, the first successful cut-price petrol company, was formed and their storage tanks at the former Southern Oil Co.'s Althorpe site on the river Trent, just above Keadby Bridge, were fed chiefly by Harkers' tanker barges, but also by those of Whitakers and Corys. So busy did the company become that barges loaded from shore-based tanks fed by Dutch and Belgian coasters either at the future site of the large APT jetty at Immingham, Killingholme or even Gunness on the Trent, and sometimes from the coasters themselves moored in the Humber off Immingham, thus resuming a practice prevalent in the 1930s that had gradually died out. By 1956, Shell had taken over Medway Oil and its craft, via Power Petrol and had *Shell Farmer* built to service their new Trentside depot at Torksey. Anglo-American Oil finally fully changed over to Esso, its American parent company's name, in 1951, and then had three craft built by Dunstons in 1956 to add to their existing *–gate* fleet

The carriage of fuel oils and lubricating oil to storage depots in the region increased markedly during the decade. These 'black oilers', built in the 1950s, were fitted with steam generators to keep the oils free-flowing and had funnels that were effectively flues for their main engine, boiler and auxiliary engines whilst the exhaust from the power units aboard white spirit vessels had to be discharged horizontally from the stern of the tanker for fear of sparks igniting the flammable vapour from their cargo tanks. For safety reasons, the latter type of vessel was not allowed to pump off its cargo if a black oiler was discharging nearby.

At this time, only the black oilers on bunkering work were equipped with radios for passing on orders, and neither radio nor radar were yet fitted aboard other tankers. However, new craft were built with crew accommodation aft so that passage between the cabin and the wheelhouse became easy and did not involve the risk of crew members struggling in adverse weather to walk along the whole length of the vessel.

A programme of mechanisation of locks on the A&CN and Trent began, thus speeding up passage of craft.

Colwick depot boomed as Harkers' larger craft delivered there and Regent opened a depot on the A&CN on the site of Fleet Mills, near Woodlesford. Petrol deliveries to Brigg, Sheffield, Newark's Farndon Field, and York ended.

This photograph, taken in Hull's St Andrew's (fish) Dock in the 1950s, features Harkers' *Mossdale H* powered by a 120hp national diesel engine and appears in the Harker Scrapbook under the heading 'Trawler Bunkering'. The passage reads:

> Each trawler takes on average 180 tons of oil. This is loaded behind Saltend jetty and is kept heated to 90 degrees Fahrenheit. A fleet of self-propelled barges is engaged on this special trade. They are equipped with VHF radio which allows them to be in continuous contact with the office controlling their movements. The bunkers are pumped into the trawler by the barge in an average time of 2/3 hours. The service is carried out for Shell Mex & BP. Mossdale H also carries a small supply of gas oil in her forward cofferdam for delivery to trawlers and use in their auxiliary engines.

Point End slipway across the canal from Harkers' yard at Knottingley, built to increase the Company's working area. (M. Bolton Collection)

Passage between the crew's cabin for'ard and the vessel's wheelhouse in rain, wind and snow could not have been a comfortable experience and this is illustrated by a photograph of Harkers' *Lonsdale H* on a stormy Humber. (M. Bolton Collection)

From the early 1930s, cod liver oil was extracted on the trawlers whilst at sea. Designated tankers based in Humber fish docks then collected it as they landed their catches and this one is moored alongside a trawler for that purpose in St Andrew's Dock, Hull.

The lighter *Murre* was built in 1929 for John A. Scott of Hull but fitted with a 170hp engine in 1953 to produce a towing tanker barge of 100 tons capacity. The vessel passed to Gilyott & Scott in 1964, on formation of that company by amalgamation of several lighter owners and is shown moored on the river Hull. (M.F. Haddon)

In 1950, Harkers built and launched from the Garlick part of their yard the Sheffield size, 100-ton capacity tanker *Sidney Billbrough* for Yorkshire Tar Distillers. The vessel was fitted with a 68hp National engine and joined *Lincoln* (see page 26) in collecting tar from York and also collecting from gasworks at Kilnhurst and Stourton for delivery to their refinery at Knottingley.

Opposite below: Several craft were built by Cook, Welton & Gemmell (CWG) in 1952–53 to Harkers' plans using some prefabricated parts lorried from a company at Bolton, Lancashire. One of these, the 132ft x 17½ft, 260-ton capacity *Ennerdale H* fitted with a 120hp Gleniffer diesel engine, is shown leaving Ocean Lock, Goole, to reload at Saltend. (Jarvis Whitton)

Above: With its aft crew accommodation evident, Harkers' fully laden 132ft x 17½ft, 220-ton capacity motor tanker *Yaredale H*, launched at Knottingley in 1950 and, fitted with a 120hp Blackstone engine, heads up the Ouse towards Goole and the A&CN. New craft were fitted with their own pumps from about this time and the pumphouse is visible immediately in front of the wheelhouse. *Yaredale H*'s were driven from its main engine.

The 138ft x 18ft, 320-ton capacity *Bannerdale H*, built by CWG in 1952 and fitted with a 152hp Gardner engine is shown penning up the new Town Lock at Newark. This vessel is typical of the new approximately 140ft-long craft that were able to deliver to Colwick after 1952. Other craft built to take advantage of the new lock at Newark were the light oil carriers *Baysdale H, Bilsdale H, Bishopdale H, Blakedale H, Bowdale H, Bransdale H, Broachdale H* and *Buckdale H*.

The 138ft x 17½ft, 250-ton capacity *Broachdale H*, fitted with a 152hp main engine, and another Harker motor tanker are shown discharging their cargoes at Colwick depot. After doing two trips to Colwick and back, crews were often expected to fit two deliveries to Jet at Althorpe into their week.

The 138ft x 17½ft, 250-ton capacity *Buckdale H*, fitted with a 160hp Gleniffer main engine, preparing to swing in the Trent after discharging its cargo of petrol at Colwick whilst on its maiden voyage in 1953. (Les Reid)

Harkers motor tanker *Yewdale H*, launched at Knottingley in 1950, is shown loading at Killingholme on the Humber's south bank near a sea-going tanker in the early days of the Jet petrol operation. This vessel and *Yaredale H* (see page 45) became cod liver oil boats in 1969. (Jarvis Whitton)

Left: Ernest Arnold (1905–1959) joined Harkers in 1920 as an office boy and rose to become joint managing director of Lyon & Lyon, the parent company. Prone to appearing at all hours in his chauffeur-driven car at canal bridges and recognised stopping places where his tankers could be found, he seemed to be universally recognised by the boatmen he supervised as single-handedly responsible for Harkers' success.

Whitakers' 129ft x 17½ft, 250-ton capacity motor tank barge *Regality* being prepared at Thorne for its 1953 launch from Dunstons' yard. *Regina E* and *Jondor* were also built here for Whitakers and these three were the first Whitaker craft to be fitted with pumps when new.

Opposite below: The 83ft x 19ft 'motor coaling lighter' *Batavia* was built by CWG at Beverley in 1924 and, after purchase by Whitakers in 1950, was re-engined by fitting a new 114hp Gardner unit and converted by YDDC to a 230-ton capacity fuel oil tanker. The recently converted craft is pictured outside its owners Lime Street wharf in 1951 with workmen again in attendance. (Whitakers)

Whitakers' 129ft x 17½ft, 250-ton capacity motor tank barge *Jondor* (see G. Chester, page 30) had its original 150hp Crossley engine replaced by a 150hp Gardner within a few years. The tanker is shown discharging fuel oil at York glassworks. Traffic here began in the 1930s, and was continued by *Lincoln* during the Second World War and maintained until 1983. (Malcolm Slater)

Opposite above: Cooks' motor tanker *Starling C*, Wivenhoe-built in 1953, approaches Knottingley glassworks whilst heading up the A&CN with a cargo for Leeds. (M. Bolton Collection)

Opposite below: Dunstons built three 123ft x 17½ft motor tankers for Esso and one of these, *Esso Leeds*, is shown heading through Goole docks, bound for its owners' Leeds depot. (John Noble Collection)

ESSO LEEDS
Esso

Above: The 1956 launch of *Esso Saltend* at Thorne is shown. *Esso Nottingham* was the other member of the trio besides *Esso Leeds.* (Norman Burnitt)

Opposite above: By 1956, the Shell-Mex & B.P. Petroleum Co., had acquired Medway Oil's craft and had had CWG build the (137ft x 29ft) 450-ton capacity *Shell Farmer* to service their new depot at Torksey. The vessel was fitted with a 324hp Lister Blackstone engine driving through a 360-degree rotatable Voith-Schneider propulsion unit instead of a rudder and is shown here fully loaded on the Humber.

Opposite below: Plans of *Shell Farmer.* (CWG)

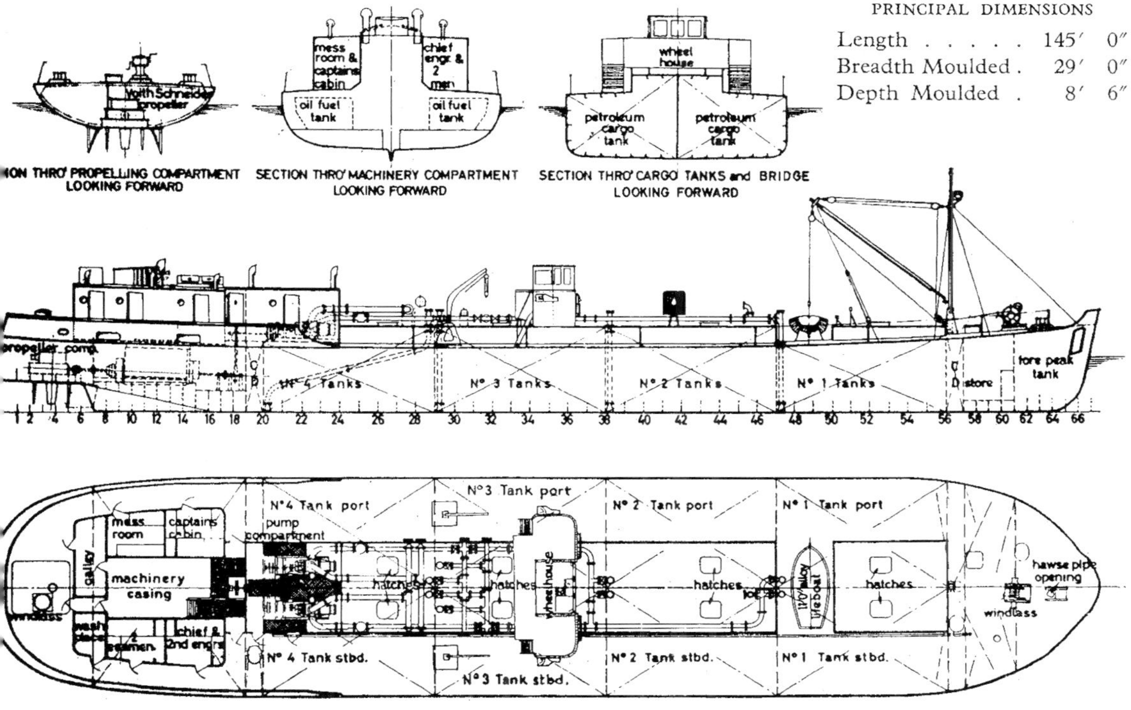

PRINCIPAL DIMENSIONS

Length	145′	0″
Breadth Moulded .	29′	0″
Depth Moulded .	8′	6″

GENERAL ARRANGEMENT OF THE 'SHELL FARMER'

Harkers built *Cordale H*, *Crossdale H*, *Coledale H* and so on as 'black oilers', fitted with heating coils to carry various grades of fuel oil and suitable for trading to Colwick. In February 1959, whilst returning from Colwick, one of these, the 230-ton capacity *Crossdale H,* did what several craft have done on the Trent when the river is in flood, and left the channel to end up stranded on the river bank after the waters had receded. This photograph was taken on the western bank, a few hundred yards above Dunham Bridge.

Bill Hodgson, Shipwright at Harkers 1929–1973

Trent boatmen used to say they could navigate using trees when both banks were under water. One of them, on *Crossdale*, couldn't and we ended up with a ship weighing a hundred tons stuck on a muddy bank forty feet from the river, well away from any road.

Everything I needed was delivered from Knottingley to Dunham Bridge by our lorry, loaded into a cog boat and pulled up to us.

When the water went away, *Crossdale* started sinking in the mud and I had to try to lift it and put launchways underneath. There wasn't a single stone in the mud which meant easy digging but when we'd got timber in place and the jacks fully up to their one foot lift, the ship had only risen about four inches.

We put a timber launchway each side, gave them a layer of tallow with soft soap on top and used the winch to pull the ship lengthways back towards the river. I'd decided to do a re-launch broadside into the river, so we had to lift the ship again, put it on blocks and shift the launchways so that they were at right-angles to the ship.

I was cautious about holding the ship as it was transferred from the blocks to the launchways, so I buried a thick post ten feet down and gave it a good lean-back. I put a wire rope from this to the ship and fastened it with a heavy cotton line. All I had to do then after removing the blocks was to chop through the cotton line and back into the water it went.

four

The 1960s

Cooks' craft were taken over by Corys in 1963 and were managed by Whitakers from 1969.

Harkers carried more fuel oil than ever before during the decade; Trent tonnages of petroleum fractions reached a peak in 1964 of 170,000 tons to Colwick, 112,000 tons to Torksey and 9,600 tons to Newark. (Division of Colwick and Newark tonnages by 200 tons, the average weight of cargo carried due to varying water levels, and Torksey tonnages by 320 tons will give some idea of the number of barge voyages involved.)

A major ten-year contract between British Waterways (BWB), Corys, Harkers and Whitakers was signed for deliveries to Esso at Leeds which involved construction (four by Harkers and two by YDDC) of six large new craft 175½ft x 18½ft having a capacity of 500 tons, fitted with 240hp Kelvin main engines. Extensive improvements of the A&CN's 'track' were also undertaken by BWB. On the down side, Jet was bought out in 1961 and their Trent depot closed in 1966, whilst Shell closed their depot at Torksey in 1967 and ended their use of the Humber waterways shortly after, having sold two of their ex-Medway Oil craft to Whitakers and two to a waterboat company.

In 1969, loading at the Saltend tanker barge jetties in Hedon Haven, was transferred to the new Associated Petroleum Terminal (APT) at Immingham and the Saltend site began its transformation to the present large petrochemical complex.

Lighterage of vegetable oils was still taking place at Hull in the 1960s and Hepworths of Paull built the 180-ton capacity dumb tanker *S&F 18* for Saner & Furley in 1954. It is shown here as *SF 20* setting off down the river Hull from a wharf above Stoneferry Bridge, when owned by Gilyott & Scott, a company which took over the lighters of several other companies in 1964. The hatch covers provide some insulation for the tanks below. (John Noble Collection)

Jack Radford, Tommy Stones and John Pettinger, Trent Tankermen

J.R.: At Colwick, petrol and black oil could not be pumped off at the same time from craft moored at a jetty because of the danger of sparks from the black oilers. This caused the racing, as well as the fact that no crew liked to be sitting aboard waiting to discharge with three or four boats ahead of them. They would still be at Colwick when the first barge was passing Stockwith on the way back. Then they'd be short of water below Cromwell. Since the crews were on a low basic wage with good trip money, they'd then have to put in extra hours to make up for delays.

T.S.: All the petrol barges going up to Colwick tried to beat each other and the black oilers. All of them had doctored the governors on their engines with a garter. The bloke on the boat in front wouldn't let anything pass if he could help it. Something might get past on the inside of a bend but then catch the bottom. It was like dodgems; if the boat in front was caught up, the second man would often drop his bow on the other man's stern and shove him right round to get past.

J.P.: We regularly ran into fog but we kept going even though none of us had radio or radar. We'd be meeting gravellers shooting past or lying across the channel grounded and waiting for water. That Jet run was even more of a rat race than Colwick. You could be meeting a ship in White Booth Roads on every tide with six or seven tankers waiting to load out of it. Then, when you got to Keadby you'd join a queue by sticking your boat on the mud because there wouldn't be enough water on the berth. As soon as you'd discharged, it'd be straight back to load again.

In the early 1960s, Whitakers decided to lengthen some craft, thereby increasing their carrying capacities. The Thorne-built *Regina E* is in a river Hull dry dock prior to insertion of a new section and an extra tank, increasing its length from 121½ft to 139ft and its carrying capacity from 250 tons to 275 tons. *Regality* was similarly treated, but the company's other Dunston-built tanker, *Jondor* was never lengthened. (Jack Radford)

Above: Harkers built both *Rebus Stone* and *Rufus Stone* for Corys in 1963. Each vessel was 132ft x 17½ft, with a capacity of 250 tons and fitted with a 150hp Gardner main engine. The latter vessel is shown leaving Goole on the A&CN, bound for Leeds. (P.L. Smith)

Harkers' 142ft x 17½ft, 320-ton capacity, Gardner-engined *Beldale H* heading up the A&CN after leaving Pollington lock, bound for Leeds with a cargo of petrol. (BWB)

Opposite below: In February 1963, Harkers' *Brocodale H* and *Blakedale H* left Goole in dense fog on the early morning tide. Both vessels ran onto the Ouse training wall at Swinefleet and the latter vessel is pictured at low water later that morning. The craft were in a much less severe predicament than *Crossdale H* (page 54) and were refloated on the afternoon tide. After returning to Goole to be checked over, they set off again for Saltend to reload. (John Noble Collection)

Above: With spectators on *Courtdale H* and the almost complete *Grovedale H*, the 61ft x 18ft *Revillio*, fitted with a 112hp main engine, is launched broadside into the A&CN at Knottingley in 1966. The name was derived from 'liver oil' and the vessel was built for Grimsby Cod Liver Oils.

Opposite above: Shell sold off their ex-Medway Oil tankers, *Mobilitie* and *Tenacitie*, in the 1960s to become water boats in 1962 and, after deliveries to Torksey ceased, *Alacritie* and *Mobilitie* to Whitakers, who also bought the three Dunston-built *Esso–* tankers (page 51 and 52) at the same time, renaming them *Humber Prince, –Princess, and –Queen*. *Alacritie*, shown on the Trent loaded with petrol for Newark, was built as a Trent size dumb boat at Hessle in 1936, motorised in 1948 and lengthened to 124ft in 1955. The vessel then had a capacity of 200 tons but only carried an average of about 170 tons on its many runs to Newark. The tanker was scrapped in 1975 after its engine seized shortly after leaving Grimsby. (John Noble)

Opposite below: Taken at London's Waldorf Hotel as the Esso Leeds contract was being signed; from left to right: Keith Whitaker of Whitakers, E.W. Hardiman of Esso, A.M. Allen of BWB and Michael Lyon of Harkers. (Whitakers)

JOHN H. WHITAKER (TANKERS) LTD. HULL.

Left: Work by BWB is in progress on a drained Bulholme lock in preparation for the new Esso Leeds traffic. The curved lock base has yet to be removed.

Below: Harkers' new 500-ton capacity *Farndale H*, 1967-built at their own yard for the Esso contract, passing the new British Waterways' Knostrop depot, opened in 1958, whilst returning from Leeds having delivered petrol to the depot there in 1968. (BWB)

Opposite below: Harkers built *Farndale H, Fossdale H, Fusedale H* and *Battle Stone* for the Esso Leeds contract, whilst the YDDC built *Humber Enterprise* and *Humber Renown*, in 1967. *Humber Enterprise* is shown pumping off at Leeds in 1978 during the tenth year of the contract.

Above: Cory's Harker-built *Battle Stone*, launched in 1968 for the Esso Leeds contract, coming up the Humber off Hull when new.

An artist's depiction of Saltend terminal taken from the 1924 edition of the Port of Hull Guide.

An aerial view, looking north, of Saltend oil jetties in 1950. No.1 jetty (right) was built in 1914, No.2 followed in 1928. Ships delivered refined petroleum products for the storage tanks here. Most tanker barges loaded at jetties in Hedon Haven, just visible to the right of this view, but fuel oil was piped aboard at berths on the shore side of the main jetties. The tank farm trebled in size before loading of craft eventually moved across the Humber. (Associated British Ports)

Immingham Oil Terminal or the Associated Petroleum Terminal (APT) opened in 1969 to receive crude oil for two refineries sited several miles away at its jetty, shown in this aerial view looking south. Some of the refineries' products are piped back to the jetty to be exported through the four barge/coaster berths on the 'finger' jetty, shown closer to the river bank, after they have been stored, if necessary, in the tanks visible. (Total)

Left: Some of the world's largest ships bring crude oil to the APT jetty, though never fully loaded. *Al Badiah*, is one such vessel. The part-loaded vessel has just tied up at its berth. APT currently handles over 25 million tons of oil and oil products each year. (Associated British Ports)

Below: Harkers' *Cotterdale H* and *Moredale H*, each of 300 tons capacity, moored at the APT oil terminal's finger jetty to load. (T. Stones)

Corys' *Rufus Stone*, *Rebus Stone* and *Battle Stone* were built for the company by Harkers at Knottingley and all have been mentioned earlier. Before constructing subsequent craft at their own Wivenhoe, Essex, yard, they had the 104ft x 21½ft *Wade Stone* built for them and fitted with a 200hp Gardner engine by Harkers in 1969. The vessel is shown on its Humber trials. The *Stone* part of these names originated from 1947 when the company took over Stone Brothers' tanker craft on the Thames. (Harkers)

Cory Tank Craft's ex-Cooks' 270-ton capacity *Redshank C*, with a 180hp main engine, was operated by Whitakers from 1969 and is shown delivering petrol at Majors' Newark depot in 1969. (John Noble Collection)

Initially, BWB used their dry cargo fleet to carry crates of imported bottled lager from Goole to Nottingham in the 1960s. As the demand grew, the lager was carried in 3-ton/500-gallon tanks, fourteen to a barge, and *Kappa B.W.* is seen approaching Owston Ferry as it heads up the Trent loaded with lager in tanks.

One of the major obstacles to smooth running of deliveries on the A&CN was flooding on the 'five-mile pond' between Castleford and Ferrybridge. Here, passage beneath the old Great North Road bridge at Ferrybridge is only just possible. (M. Bolton Collection)

five

The 1970s and 1980s

Waterborne deliveries to Colwick depot ended in 1971, beaten by underground pipelines and rail transport.

Whitakers decided to end their dry cargo work on the waterways in the early 1970s and converted three of their craft to tankers. However, in March 1976, Harkers ceased to carry on the Humber waterways, having run down their fleet there from thirty tankers in 1970 to fifteen in 1975. Whitakers bought nine of their craft and six Cory Tank Craft that they had been managing for seven years, and also took over the work that they had been doing, thus making them the biggest carriers of petroleum liquids on UK waterways, delivering over a million tons a year. They reopened Fleet storage depot in 1976, after forming Whitfleet as a subsiduary, and, in the following year, their YDDC started building a series of six sophisticated 200ft x 19½ft tanker barges of 650 tons capacity, fitted with either 320hp Kelvin or Lister or 365hp Cummins main engines, plus bow thrusters, radar, ship to ship radio, hydraulic lever steering and retractable wheelhouses. Four were built for the parent company and two for Whitfleet between 1977 and 1983. Whitakers' deliveries to Esso, Leeds ended in 1982 but they then began bringing fuel oil to power stations such as High Marnham on the Trent, Drax on the Ouse, Thorpe Marsh near the S&SYN at Barnby Dun and Ferrybridge on the A&CN. The long-established oil traffic to York glassworks, however, ended in 1983. There was a resurgence in the imported tar deliveries from Goole to Knottingley, but these faded out in the late 1980s.

J.R. Rix & Sons of Hull had also bought three of Harkers' tankers in the 1970s and began to use them to deliver chiefly to sites on the river Hull.

Meanwhile, in 1975, a less pleasant traffic had begun on the Humber waterways, after Effluent Services had purchased an ex-Harker tanker and five other tankers from Rotterdam to carry effluent from sewage works at Sandall on the S&SYN and Knostrop on the A&CN to Goole, for onward disposal at sea. A further ex-Harker tanker was purchased by the company in 1976. Effluent Services ceased to operate their craft by mid-1981, Dave Cook of Hedon's fleet of second-hand craft taking over. Eventually the traffic passed to Dean & Dyball who bought two 1959-built French tankers for the inland waterway part of the operation and a coaster for disposal of the material at sea.

By the end of the 1970s, ship to shore radio had been fitted to most tankers; vessels built in the 1960s were under conversion to hydraulic steering, and radar was being installed in craft or portable radar sets were being brought aboard, though ship to ship VHF radio had to wait until the 1990s for blanket coverage. Harkers built their last inland waterway tanker at Knottingley, *Conveyor*, in 1979 but continued to offer a ship repair facility. Dunstons had built their last tanker, *Esso Saltend*, as early as 1956, their last vessel at Thorne in 1980, and left the town in 1987 to concentrate on the Henry Scarr yard at Hessle that they had actually taken over in 1931.

Opposite above: Whitakers' 124ft x 19½ft *Humber Navigator* was built by YDDC in 1964 as a dry cargo barge and lengthened to 142ft in 1968. In 1973, however, the owners decided to convert it (and *Sirwin* and *Keewhit*) to tankers. The 350-ton capacity tanker passes up Newark dyke to deliver a cargo of petrol to the nearby depot.

Opposite below: Effluent Services' 290-ton capacity *Sandall* (ex-*Breckondale H*) immediately after it had left Pollington lock, bound for Goole.

JOHN H WHITAKER TANKERS LTD HULL.

SANDALL
COOLE

Effluent Services' 245-ton capacity ex-mainland European waterway tanker *Balby* in Knottingley cutting whilst en route for Goole in 1978.

Effluent Services' *Millshaw* (ex-*Rosette* of Rotterdam) and *Sandall* trans-shipping their offensive cargoes to the sea-going vessel *Anglezarke* prior to its disposal at sea.

Northern Counties Carriers' 1930s-built Leeds & Liverpool 'shortboat' *Irwell* was fitted with a 55-ton capacity cylindrical tank and used to bring effluent to Knostrop from Esholt Sewage works, 9 miles and fifteen 62ft-long locks above Leeds. On occasions in 1979, as when this picture was taken, as it approached Fishpond lock, the vessel took a cargo all the way down the A&CN to Goole for trans-shipment.

Anon, Skipper of an effluent barge

Those continental barges were more concrete than steel when we got them. They were real rust buckets and had more patches on their hulls than I've ever known. Nudge any obstacle, however gently, when on the move and there'd be another leak. Then, someone would have to do one of the most disgusting jobs on earth and go down into the tanks after pumping off, find the hole and fix it!

Some of the men aboard were no better. There were some right cowboys on this job and no one seemed to check up on them. I've known crews bring a full load to Goole, pump off only part of it into the coaster and take the rest back to Knostrop. Then they'd top up there and come back to Goole, saving hours at both ends. When they wanted to save any more time, they'd only part-load at Knostrop and top up with canal water after they'd set off back to Goole. Even one of the coaster skippers was on the fiddle. They were supposed to dump the stuff miles out in the North Sea, but he was prosecuted for pumping off as he passed Spurn.

There was an awful stench over most of the docks as we trans-shipped at Goole and it got onto our clothing. After complaints, the company issued us with gallons of rose water to sprinkle on ourselves when we used public transport to travel home from the boat.

Whitakers' ex-Harker, 250-ton capacity tanker *Brocodale H* prepares to tie up at the tanker berth at Wakefield to deliver a cargo of fuel oil.

Whitakers' ex-Harker tanker *Marchdale H* loading tar at Goole from the coaster *Theodore* in 1979.

Three of Whitakers' ex-Harker tankers *Marchdale H, Moredale H and Cotterdale H* bringing tar loaded from a ship at Goole to the former Aire Tar works on Bank Dole Cut, Knottingley, in 1979.

Whitakers' Humber Tanker Fleet, 1978

Light Oils		**Heavy Oils**
LOW FLASH		
Berriedale	*Battle Stone*	*Blackbird*
Fossdale	*Fusedale*	*Cotterdale*
Humber Enterprise	*Humber Jubilee*	*Humber Fueller*
Humber Mariner	*Humber Navigator*	*Humber Dawn*
Humber Renown	*Regality*	*Jondor*
Rebus Stone	*Rufus Stone*	*Marchdale*
Sirwin		*Moredale*
HIGH FLASH		*Newdale*
Brocodale	*David W*	MOTOR TUG
Fidelitie	*Humber Princess*	*Cawood*
Humber Star	*Keewhit*	DUMB TANK BARGES
Regina E	*Rienzi*	*A.A.Simpson*
Tadcaster	*Wheatcroft*	*T.P.Bullard*
MOBILE STEAMING UNIT		*Lysbeth*
Coalite		

Whitfleet tankers
Farndale, Dunlin, Redshank Seagull

The list includes ex-Harker and ex-Cory craft acquired by Whitakers in 1976 with *H* dropped from the Harker names and *C* dropped from the Cook and Cory names, though, as may be seen from photographs near this point in the book, the actual names painted on the craft occasionally retained these letters.

Above: Two of Rix & Sons' lengthened ex-Harker tankers, *Burdale H* and *Beldale H*, with a capacity of 390 tons but still retaining their original 152hp Gardner main engines, waiting for water between Hull's Drypool and North bridges before delivering their cargoes of petrol from Immingham to wharves on the river Hull in the early 1980s.

By the 1970s, D. Cook (Hedon) had added *Ryedale H* and *Wheldale H* to his fleet. The two ex-Harker craft took over from Effluent Supplies in carrying effluent, brought to Goole from Knostrop, 12 miles out to sea, and also collected effluent from the ill-fated nylon plant at Flixborough on the Trent for similar disposal. Being essentially inland waterway craft, the tankers were often weatherbound by fog or rough seas. *Ryedale H* is shown in Goole's South Dock trailing its cargo-discharge pipe, prior to penning down into the Ouse and heading for the North Sea. (Waterways World)

Opposite below: In the 1960s, D. Cook of Hedon had bought three tankers, *S.T. Morgan*, *Onward Pioneer* and *Regent Linnet*, a 92ft x 18½ft former Severn petrol carrier built in 1951 by Yarwoods of Northwich. He never acquired a spirit licence for the craft, but they did some bunkering at Grimsby, Immingham and Saltend and even managed a few cargoes to York and up Hull Harbour. *Regent Linnet* also carried some gas oil. It is shown here in 1982, ready for scrapping at Carlton wharf on the Trent, though it was rescued and eventually became a crane boat. (J. Noble Collection)

Above: The first of six new sophisticated, 650-ton capacity tankers built at Hull, Whitakers' *Humber Jubilee*, launched at YDD in 1977 and fitted with a 320hp main engine, waits to complete penning up through Goole's Ocean lock alongside their ex-Harker vessel *Marchdale H* in 1979. *Jubilee* was bound for Leeds, *Marchdale* for Wakefield. Of the over one million tons carried annually by Whitakers on the Humber waterways, half of this amount went on the A&CN to Leeds.

Whitfleet's blue and white painted fleet contained the one-time Cook barges *Redshank C*, *Dunlin C* and *Seagull C* from Cory Tank Lighterage and *Farndale H* from Harkers, in addition to the two new vessels *Fleet Enterprise* and *Fleet Endeavour* shown here in 1987 leaving Fleet depot, near Leeds. *Fleet Enterprise* was the last of the six 650-ton capacity 'supertankers', built for Whitfleet in 1983 and fitted with a 320hp Kelvin main engine.

Opposite below: Whitakers' second 'supertanker' *Humber Pride* demonstrates its retractable wheelhouse as it passes beneath Thwaite Mills bridge in 1979 whilst returning from Leeds. The Immingham–Leeds job involved a thirty-six-hour round trip and sometimes three trips were made in a week. More usually, however, the crew moored at Goole or Hull for one night after loading, going home that night and back the following morning by car, and slept aboard for two nights.

Revillio (see page 60) at work in Grimsby fish dock as a bunkering oil barge for the Exnor Co. in 1979.

The 180-ton capacity tanker lighters *O 18* and *Hen* are loading vegetable oil from the coaster *PL Trader* during 1982 in Hull's Albert Dock. Their owners, Gilyott & Scott, had forty-six lighters at the time, seven of which were tankers (including the motorised *Murre*, see page 43). Lighterage had almost ceased at Hull by this date.

Cory's *Druid Stone* was lengthened by 40ft at YDDC's dry dock in 1977. Two new 150hp Gardner engines were also fitted and the vessel became Whitakers' 400-ton capacity *Humber Dawn*. The tanker is rounding Morton Corner on the Trent, bound for High Marnham power station in 1984, with a cargo of fuel oil; a traffic that began in 1983.

Whitakers ex-Cory, ex-Cook 220-ton capacity tanker *Blackbird C*, built at Wivenhoe in 1959, turning in the Ouse at York after delivering a cargo of fuel oil to glassworks on the Foss.

Deliveries by water to Colwick depot resumed in 1987 for a few years and Whitakers' 1978-lengthened ex-Whitfleets', ex-Corys', ex-Cooks', 260-ton capacity tanker *Seagull*, 1960-built at Wivenhoe, is shown at Gunthorpe coming back down the Trent after delivering 'oil products' (according to a relevant press release) there. The vessel was extensively refurbished for this traffic by YDDC in 1986.

Opposite above: Whitakers' ex-Harker 125ft x 21ft, 350-ton capacity tanker *Newdale H* bunkering North Sea Ferries' *Norwave* in King George Dock, Hull, in 1980.

Opposite below: Three Whitaker tankers, *Humber Dawn*, *Brocodale H* and *Marchdale H*, bunkering a large freighter in Hull's King George Dock. (Whitakers)

NORTH SEA FERRIES

Left: In 1986, YDDC converted the 1976-built, 1,000-ton capacity coaster *Wilks* to the tanker *Teesdale H* for Whitakers. The 149ft x 21ft, twin-screw vessel, powered by two 365hp Caterpillar engines is shown later that year heading up the Ouse above Boothferry Bridge, bound for Drax power station with a cargo of fuel oil. The *H* suffix was used because the vessel was to be sent to the Tyne/Tees region where Whitakers had continued to operate under the John Harker name. (Whitakers)

Below: The beginning of the end of the effluent traffic is represented as the final carrier starts work on the contract in 1987. Dean & Dyball's tanker barge *Trentaire* transships its cargo to their coaster *Reedness* at Goole for disposal at sea. *Trentcal* was the company's other 180ft x 16½ft inland waterway vessel.

six

The 1990s to date

By the early 1990s, traffic in fuel oil on the Ouse, Trent, S&SYN and the Wakefield branch of the A&CN, had dwindled away. By contrast, at the turn of the century, Rix & Sons were building new vessels at the former Hepworth shipyard at Paull, acquired in the 1980s. They were also delivering petrol up Hull Harbour and bunkering with their refurbished and renamed ex-Harker tankers, converted dry cargo coasters and craft built at Paull. Whitakers were still bunkering and won a new contract to carry oil to Rotherham.

Dean & Dyball's disposal of effluent at sea was finally phased out in 1997, on environmental grounds.

Harkers, having built over 100 tankers at Knottingley, not all for themselves and some for themselves that were destined to be based away from the Humber waterways in the Mersey, Severn and Tyne/Tees areas, continued as a boatyard doing repairs until 1990. They then withdrew, the yard was renamed 'Fernley Green Industrial Estate', and split up into small units for rental by firms, most of which had no interest in the adjacent canal. Dunstons' Henry Scarr yard at Hessle built its last tanker, *Bisley*, for Bowker & King in 1969, closed in 1994, but then opened a ship repair service at Hull's William Wright Dock and this is still in existence. YDDC built its final tanker barge, *Fleet Enterprise*, in 1983 and closed in 1997, having built twenty-four tanker barges, five of which were originally dry cargo craft.

One of the last tanker lighterages at Hull occurred in April 2000 as the ex-Thames lighter *Lugsail* loaded 275 tons of maize oil for delivery up the harbour. It was taken up the river Hull by Dean's Tugs' *Gillian Knight*, moving stern first as shown on this view taken below Drypool Bridge.

The 400-ton capacity *Rix Osprey* (ex-*Beldale H*), lengthened at Knottingley in 1978 and converted to a black oiler in 1999, loading 350 tons of imported talloil (a Swedish liquidised woodpulp product, able to be used as a substitute for fuel oil) brought by road tanker from nearby storage tanks at Immingham in 2004. Of Rix's other two ex-Harker tankers, *Burtondale H*, lengthened and widened at Paull, became the 540-ton capacity *Rix Falcon* and *Burdale H* became the 400-ton capacity clean oiler *Rix Kestrel*. (Mike Brown)

Having built the new tanker *Rix Eagle* at Paull in 1990 and lengthened it in 1996 to give it a capacity of 650 tons, Rix & Sons also built the 200ft x 19½ft, 600-ton capacity *Rix Owl*, at Paull in 2002. The tanker, fitted with a 350hp Caterpillar engine and a bow thruster, is shown passing Blacktoft on the Ouse in 2003 with a cargo of gas oil and kerosene for Butlers' depot at Castleford on the A&CN.

Dave Hill, Skipper of *Rix Osprey*

We make radio contact with the Piermaster as we approach Immingham Oil Terminal and a tug is sent to us to be on standby as we drop onto our berth. It comes alongside as we tie up. A 'jetty man' helps us with mooring and also sets valves for loading, as well as taking samples as we load and watching for any problems that may arise. With full personal protective equipment, that is lifejackets, hard hats, gloves and glasses, one of us climbs onto the jetty to see the Cargo Inspector and then runs through the safety checklist with him. The loading form agreeing on the grade and amounts of cargo to be pumped into each tank is then completed and they then come back aboard and our tanks are checked for any contamination.

Loading starts and the cargo is metered into our tanks, with two of us on watch to make sure that we inform the jetty man when we estimate that it is about ten minutes before we are fully loaded. He telephones the Cargo Superintendent at control, about half a mile away, and delivery will stop when complete, unless we need to stop short for some reason, in which case we tell the jetty man and he hits a button which stops loading in approximately fifteen seconds. An Independent Surveyor then dips the tanks before checking his figures against those of the oil terminal's surveyor and sealing the cargo if they agree.

With the Berthing Master overseeing things, the jetty man throws off our ropes and the tug stands by as we leave. Bills of Lading, which used to be essential until a few years ago, are probably now sent by email. Also, a few years ago, fuel tax and VAT was charged on the cargo delivered when it left the inland depot, but now it is charged before it leaves the oil terminal. Therefore another Independent Surveyor appears at the depot where we are discharging and, taking into account the temperature difference between loading and discharge points, checks that we are delivering all that was loaded.

Rix Osprey has two three-man crews, each working twenty-four/seven on alternate weeks. Younger members of the crews now go on courses covering safety and survival at sea, first aid, use of radar, VHF and digital selective calling. In my day, I learned these by experience and from watching others. Drunkeness, once tolerated, now leads to immediate dismissal and so does the use of drugs. Anyone aboard who is likely to navigate a tanker on the Humber has to have seen ABP, get a pilots' exemption certificate and be given a personal access number for the pilots' website. I went on a course and sat a certificate of competence that, at present, allows me to skipper a ship less than sixty metres (197ft) long and under 500 gross registered tonnes (492 tons) 30 miles from any UK port.

Just as Whitakers had converted a coaster into the tanker *Teesdale H* (see page 84), Rix & Sons purchased two similar YDDC-built dry cargo ships and produced the 1000-ton capacity tankers *Rix Hawk* (from *Wis*) and *Rix Harrier* (from *Wib*) at Paull. The latter vessel, powered by twin 365hp Caterpillar engines, is shown in the Humber off Immingham in the late 1990s loaded with bunkering oil.

Rix Merlin, the UK's newest inland waterway tanker, ready to be launched at Paull in September 2005. (Dave Hill)

After floating off the slipway at Paull, *Rix Merlin* was taken to Hull's Alexandra Dock where it is shown being fitted out. Externally, the tanker seems to have some similarity to earlier Harker vessels, apart from compliance with current regulations in having crews' accommodation on, rather than below, deck. The height of the superstructure aft would seem to rule out passage beneath any canal bridges. Below deck, however, *Rix Merlin* is a state-of-the-art, double-skinned ship with space between the outsides of tanks and the hull and completely closed-in cargo space. The tanker is fitted with a 650hp Cummins diesel engine. It made its maiden voyage in the final days of 2005.

Selby Paradigm, here photographed from Boothferry Bridge control room in 2001, was constructed as a 550-ton capacity tanker by Lincoln & Hull Marine at their Browns' dry dock in 2000 from the 150ft x 28ft graveller *Swinderby* and used to deliver rapeseed and linseed oils from BOCM's Unitrition division at Selby to Hull. The vessel was replaced after some months when it proved unreliable. It has since been sold and had its original name reinstated.

Whitakers *Humber Energy*, formerly *Fleet Enterprise*, entering Mexborough top lock whilst on its way to deliver over 500 tons of fuel oil to Green Line Oils of Rotherham in 2004.

seven

Boatyards

Readers will look here in vain for mention of some of the region's more famous shipbuilders, such as Cochranes of Selby, Goole Shipbuilding & Repairing Co. and Earles of Hull. All of these companies specialised, almost exclusively, in the construction of sea-going craft. Similarly, the builders of wooden inland waterway vessels are not mentioned because they produced few tanker barges.

Most tanker barges were built for the Humber waterways by the companies of Richard Dunston at Thorne, Henry Scarr at Hessle (bought by Dunstons in 1931), John Harker at Knottingley and the Yorkshire Dry Dock at Hull. Several tankers were built by Cooks of Wivenhoe in Essex, for James W. Cook and, later, Corys. Cook, Welton & Gemmell at Beverley also built some and a few came from J.S. Watson (Gainsborough) at Beckingham. All these yards eventually moved away from inland waterway craft to construction of fishing vessels, tugs or other non-tanker activity before going out of business. This also happened at the Hepworth shipyard at Paull, near Hull, but since being acquired by J.R. Rix & Sons, the yard has been reactivated, new vessels constructed and the company's fleet repaired and maintained here. This is the only boatyard in the UK that is currently building cargo-carrying inland waterway craft.

Apart from the earliest tankers, made by dropping tanks into dry cargo craft, effectively producing double-skinned vessels, almost all tanker barges built in the twentieth century were single-skinned. Rix's latest vessel, *Rix Merlin*, represents a return to double-skinned tankers.

This aerial view from 1952, looking approximately east, of Dunstons' yard alongside the Stainforth & Keadby Canal at Thorne, shows craft under construction and being fitted out. (Laurie Thorp)

Dunstons' yard at Thorne, also in the 1950s, viewed from the company's boardroom with inland waterway craft under construction.

Tankers were fitted with wooden cog boats until well into the 1970s and these are shown under construction at Dunstons' yard in the early twentieth century. They were propelled by sculling (using an oar at the stern) and served as a lifeboat to gain access between the moored tanker and the shore and to assist in rope and anchor handling.

A view of Henry Scarr's boatbuilding yard at Hessle (left). Part of Dobson Bros 1902–06 (Livingstone & Cooper 1906–22) may be seen on the opposite (western) bank of Hessle Haven and this dates the picture.

An aerial view, looking roughly north west, of the former Scarrs' yard in the 1960s after it had been renamed as Dunstons' in the 1950s. Construction of mainly sea-going craft seems to be taking place. Clive Sullivan Way, a dual carriageway road, has since been built between the site of the yard and the railway.

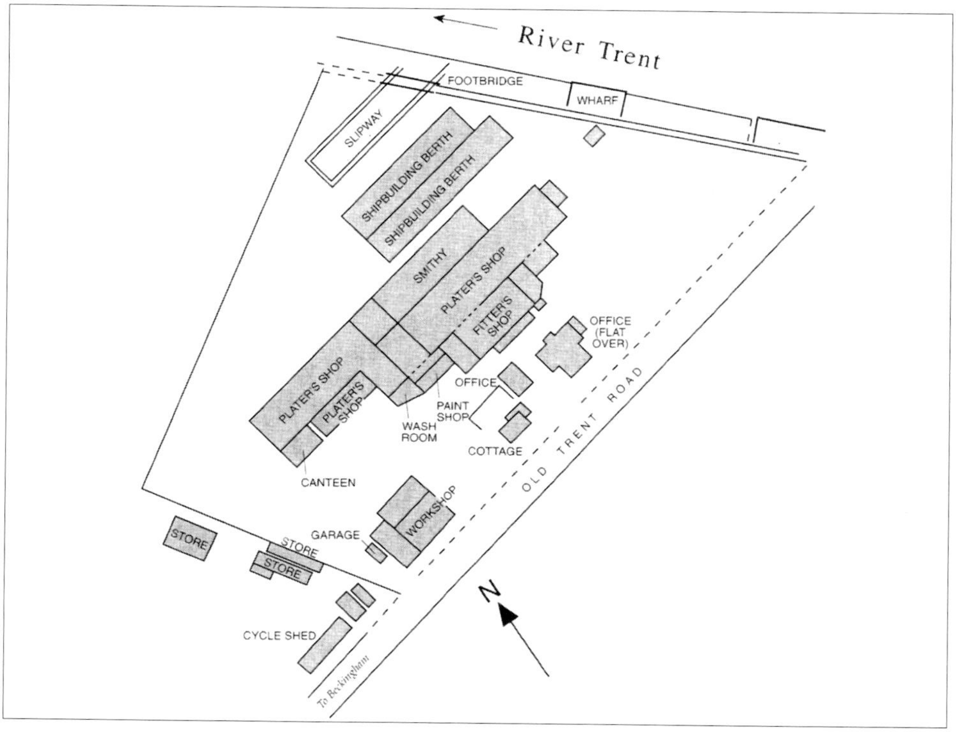

A plan of Watsons' 3-acre site at Beckingham, Lincolnshire, with 520ft of river Trent frontage, taken from the 1962 catalogue auctioning the premises.

A view of Watsons' Trent frontage from the river, taken as an aegre passes. Construction of a roof over the slipway is under way in this 1920s photograph.

An aerial view of Harkers from the late 1950s. Skew Bridge is just off right, Aimwell Place has been demolished, leaving the two former yards looking as one. Furthest from the camera, a couple of tankers are out of the water on Point End maintenance and repair slipway, which had been constructed on the opposite bank of the A&CN from the main yard. The yard underwent considerable reconstruction in 1960–61 with buildings appearing including one on the site of the former Worfolks' dry dock. As longer craft were built, broadside launchings from Worfolks site became the norm.

Opposite above: With covering of the slipway nearly complete, the tanker barge *Sealand* (see page 22) lies under construction at Watsons' yard in the late 1920s. Tanker barges were built here to carry petrol, oil and water for both Humber and Thames owners and for operation in other parts of the world.

Opposite below: An aerial view of Harkers' yard in the 1930s, taken from above Skew Bridge on the A&CN, showing the two component yards which made up the premises. The former Worfolks' yard (at the bottom of the picture) is adjacent to the bridge (not shown) and still separated from the former Garlicks' yard by the terraced houses of Aimwell Place. Two craft were often built side-by-side at this latter part of the yard to be launched lengthways. (Ron Gosney Collection)

Arthur Potts, Draughtsman at Knottingley

The manager of Harkers' yard moved there from Dunstons when it opened. He brought my father with him as yard foreman and also persuaded both Dunstons' best plater and best blacksmith to join him. I joined the company as an apprentice in 1939 and finished in 1987 as chief draughtsman, three years before the yard closed.

Procedures at the yard when I started were similar to those adopted by shipbuilders producing much larger craft. Draughtsmen drew the plans and ordered the steel which then came to Knottingley by road or rail from Scunthorpe or Teesside. Loftsmen drew out the plans to full size on the loft floor and then made the templates. The chief shipwright then laid the keel where the vessel was to be built, taking great care that it was level. The steel was delivered close to the dimensions we had ordered but the platers cut it to the exact size we required on a shearing machine and then either rolled and bent it for simple shape changes or, for more complex shapes, heated it in a furnace before hammering it into shape. They then punched the plate edges before riveters put them into place on frames made by boilermakers. These had been fastened to the keel and caulkers made overlapping plates watertight by compressing the seams with a square-edged tool. The mid-sections of the vessel were made first, then the bow and stern built on, each fitted with a tank to hold water ballast.

The foreman shipwright then took over and, four or five days before the event, prepared for launch of the tanker by building five timber launchways for a broadside entry into the water and two for an end-on entry. His final test of the tanker before launching was to put extra blocks beneath it and fill the tanks with 100 tons of water to test for leaks.

Once in the water, fitting out began, involving a blacksmith who made deck stanchions, pipe fitters, joiners, who built the accommodation, electricians and fitters who installed machinery, including engines.

Throughout building, we were visited almost weekly by inspectors from Lloyds or various departments of the Ministry of Transport, looking at adherence to plans that had been originally passed, engineering quality, safety features, or standards of accommodation.

The major change during my time was the switch to welding which began to replace riveting during the Second World War. After the war, we built the bows and sterns of tankers and welded these onto the 15 to 20ft cargo sections delivered by lorry that had been built in Lancashire and assembled here. We also built several craft from the same plans, thus cutting costs. In 1960, the yard was reorganised with introduction of all-electric machinery and construction of several new buildings. We then part-built half a vessel in the new welding shops and took it out into the yard to weld it to the other half.

We were very busy in the 1950s and 1960s with repairs and maintenance, lengthening of craft, fitting motors to dumb vessels and converting our smaller tank barges to dry cargo craft prior to selling them on. All this was done concurrently with building new vessels.

A young rivet heater stands close to some foot-powered bellows in the 1930s, ready to throw a hot rivet to a catcher who will deliver it to the riveter.

A caulker at work in Harkers' yard in the 1950s. (Harkers)

Transverse and longitudinal sections of tanks in place at Knottingley during the building of a new tanker.

Broadside launches became more prevalent at Knottingley as longer craft were built and they were always more spectacular than end-on launches where a vessel merely slid down a slipway. The launch of *Fusedale H*, in 1968, illustrates a broadside entry into the canal.

The broadside launch of *Beldale H* at Knottingley in September 1959 was spectacular, as shown, for the wrong reasons and *Esso Saltend* can be seen squeezing past the obstruction caused. Management orders to use timber damaged during a previous launch backfired as a piece broke off and became jammed beneath the stern of the tanker, thus arresting its movement.

After several hours in the position shown above, *Beldale H*'s launch was completed by pulling its bow into the bank, thus levering the stern into the water, as shown.

Left: A 120hp Blackstone diesel main engine being craned aboard the recently launched *Northdale H* at Harkers' yard in 1950. A Lister diesel auxiliary engine and an oil-fired Cochran boiler, supplying steam for the cargo pump and cargo-heating coils, were also installed.

Below: Harkers' tanker barge *Blakedale H* being fitted out after its launch at Cook, Welton & Gemmell's yard at Grovehill, Beverley, in 1952. A 152hp Gleniffer main engine was installed.

An aerial view, looking south, of the CWG yard on the river Hull at Grovehill, Beverley, in the late 1940s. Several inland waterway tankers were built here earlier in the century but, at this time, fishing vessels were its speciality though some tankers were built for Harkers in the early 1950s. Barmston Drain lies to the right of the yard. (Derek Grindell Collection)

A view, looking east, over YDDC's Lime Street yard on the river Hull. (Whitakers)

Right: A mid-1950s view of YDDC's Lime Street premises showing the dry cargo barge, later tanker barge *Keewhit*, under construction and three tanks in the floating dry dock sitting on the river Hull's muddy 'hard-standing'. The tanks would be scaled and cleaned and joints then smeared with soap solution before being tested for leaks with air under pressure prior to refitting them into the lighter from which they had been removed. This was a more convenient method of testing than the water test described in Arthur Potts' passage on page 100. (Whitakers)

Below: Construction of Whitakers' *Humber Enterprise* nears completion at YDDC's Lime Street yard early in 1967. (Whitakers)

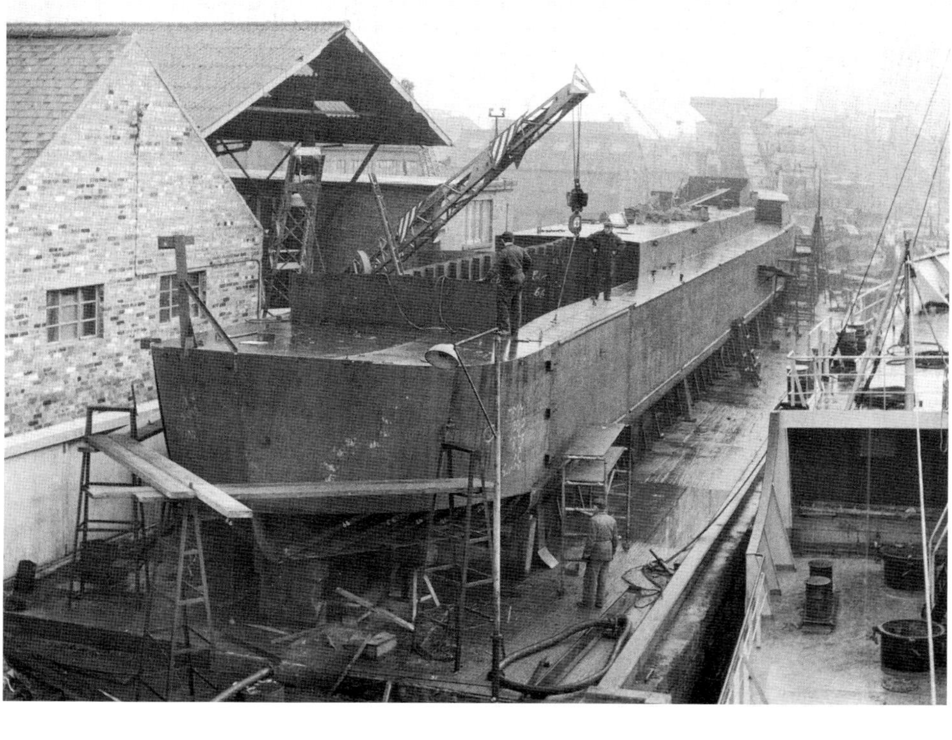

The night-time launch of Whitfleet's *Fleet Endeavour* at YDD in 1981. Months before completion of a vessel, tidal data would be used to fix a date and time for the broadside launch on a spring tide where the fall from its building berth to the river would be no more than 6ft. (Whitakers)

Right: The plan and data side of a publicity sheet published by YDDC relating to their *Fleet Enterprise*, launched in 1983. W B represents water ballast. (Whitakers)

Below: An aerial view, looking east, of Hull's North Bridge and the river Hull. The three dry docks on the nearer bank were acquired by YDDC in 1976 and used mainly for fitting out vessels built at Lime Street. The central dock (No.2), containing two vessels side by side, was formerly the entrance lock to Queen's Dock. (Whitakers)

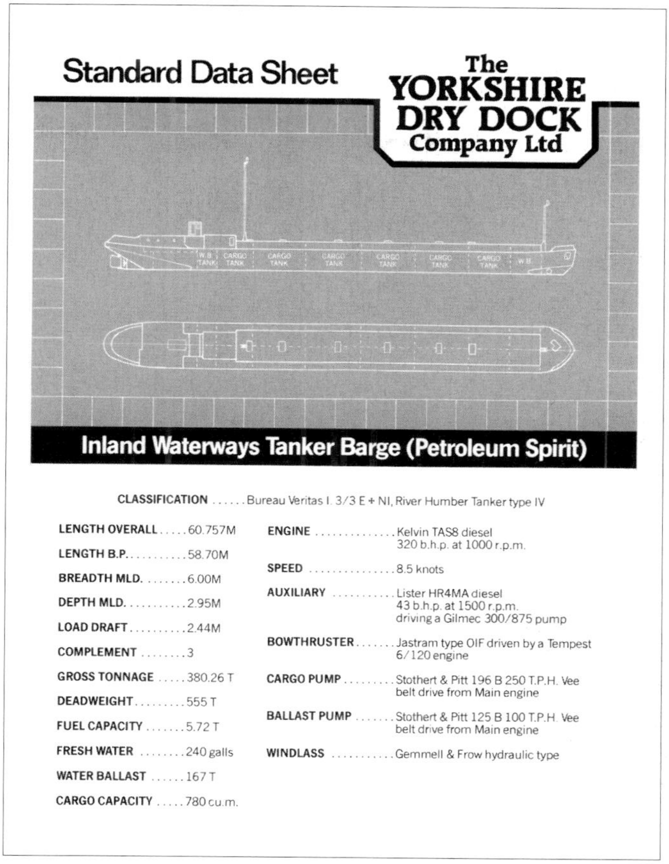

Standard Data Sheet

The YORKSHIRE DRY DOCK Company Ltd

Inland Waterways Tanker Barge (Petroleum Spirit)

CLASSIFICATION ...... Bureau Veritas I. 3/3 E + NI, River Humber Tanker type IV

LENGTH OVERALL	60.757M
LENGTH B.P.	58.70M
BREADTH MLD.	6.00M
DEPTH MLD.	2.95M
LOAD DRAFT	2.44M
COMPLEMENT	3
GROSS TONNAGE	380.26 T
DEADWEIGHT	555 T
FUEL CAPACITY	5.72 T
FRESH WATER	240 galls
WATER BALLAST	167 T
CARGO CAPACITY	780 cu.m.

ENGINE	Kelvin TAS8 diesel 320 b.h.p. at 1000 r.p.m.
SPEED	8.5 knots
AUXILIARY	Lister HR4MA diesel 43 b.h.p. at 1500 r.p.m. driving a Gilmec 300/875 pump
BOWTHRUSTER	Jastram type OIF driven by a Tempest 6/120 engine
CARGO PUMP	Stothert & Pitt 196 B 250 T.P.H. Vee belt drive from Main engine
BALLAST PUMP	Stothert & Pitt 125 B 100 T.P.H. Vee belt drive from Main engine
WINDLASS	Gemmell & Frow hydraulic type

Above: The ex-Corys' *Wade Stone*, soon to become Whitakers' *Humber Star* (being lengthened by 40ft in 1977) at YDDC's No.2 Dry Dock on High Street, Hull, as Whitakers' recently-launched *Humber Jubilee* is fitted out. (Whitakers)

Rix Falcon in dry dock at Paull in 1996. The tanker (ex-*Burtondale H*) was being lengthened and widened and, to ensure the best grant, a completely new mid-section was built and the old bows and stern welded onto it. Ten years later the bows and stern were in need of replacement, probably attracting another grant. (Dave Hill)

Opposite below: Construction of the tanker lighter *O 18* for Oldridges is in progress at Hepworths' Shipyard, Paull, in 1954.

The stern section of *Rix Merlin* under construction at Paull in 2005. (Dave Hill)

The bow section of *Rix Merlin* under construction at MMS Ship Repair & Dry Dock Co.'s Alexandra dock premises in 2005. The completed vessel is pictured on pages 89 and 90, the two sections having been welded together at Hull. (Dave Hill)

Lincoln & Hull Marine Contractors' large Trent graveller *Swinderby* leaving Keadby on the Trent for Hull with a 500-ton plus cargo of gravel in 1993. The vessel was converted to a tanker and renamed *Selby Paradigm* (see page 91) at the yard of its early owners in 2001.

Opposite above: Whitakers' dry cargo barge *Sirwin*, seen leaving Girton quarry after loading aggregate for Hull, was converted by YDDC to a tanker barge in 1973. (John Noble)

Opposite below: The YDDC-built coaster *Wilks* undergoing trials on the Humber when new, in 1976. The vessel returned to its builder's yard in 1986 to be converted into the tanker *Teesdale H* (see page 84). Similarly, the twin screw coaster *Wis* was launched by YDDC in 1976 and became *Breydon Venture* in 1986, but was then purchased by Rix & Sons and converted into the tanker *Rix Hawk* in 1996. (Whitakers)

J.J. Tomlinson's *Richard MT* (ex-Harkers' *Jim H*) was sold and converted to a dry cargo barge in 1953. It is seen crossing West Dock, Goole. (Norman Burnitt)

Above: The converted ex-Harker tanker *Annie H* leaving Thorne lock in 1983 with a cargo of Trent aggregate for Knottingley.

Right: The converted ex-Harker tanker *Dorothy H* tying up at Queen's Staithe, York, with a bulk dry cargo load.

LANDRAIL C.
LANDRA

John Branford's *Eskdale* (built at Knottingley in 1946) and *Mossdale* (built at Knottingley in 1949, see page 41) at Doncaster wharf in 1971 as a new gravel wharf was being built at East Butterwick on the Trent for what became a very successful operation in carrying Lincolnshire sand to glassworks at Knottingley. Harkers sold the craft in 1968 and 1971, respectively, after they themselves had converted them to dry cargo craft. (John Branford)

Opposite above: The former Cooks' Dunston-built dumb tanker *Landrail C*, converted by Hepworths of Paull in 1963 to a motorised dry cargo barge, approaching Newark after delivering a dry cargo to Nottingham. (Les Reid)

Opposite below: Three former Harker tankers which were sold and converted to dry cargo vessels in the 1950s and early 1960s, are shown after discharging grain at Carlton wharf on the Trent when owned by a Barton-on-Humber carrier. *Sutton A* (ex-*Barnsdale H*) is on the right, in the centre is *Carlton A* (ex-*Patterdale H*) and at the rear is *Janet A* (original name). (John Noble Collection)

CORDALE
BAYSDALE

PROGRESS

All six of the craft built for the Esso Leeds contract in the mid-1960s (see pages 61–63) have been converted to dry cargo craft and most of them are currently being used for delivering Trent aggregate from Besthorpe to Whitwood on the A&CN. The former Cory Tank Craft's *Battle Stone* is shown in 2003, after conversion by its new owners, Lafarge, in Hessle Haven with a cargo of sand being discharged by grab onto a heap on the site once occupied by Henry Scarr's boatyard.

Opposite above: In 1984, John Branford bought the former effluent carrier *Knostrop*, converted it to a dry cargo carrier and gave the vessel back its original name, *Baysdale* (built by CWG at Beverley in 1952), in line with the names of the rest of his fleet at the time. The vessel is shown on the Ouse, approaching Goole's Victoria Lock, under tow by his *Cordale* (built at Knottingley in 1956).

Opposite below: Progress (ex-*Ennerdale H*, see page 45) in Waddingtons' yard at Swinton in the mid-1980s, after purchase by that company in 1979. The vessel had been converted from a tanker in 1974 and was the first craft longer than 61ft to pass so far up the improved S&SYN in 1980. The company also bought *Lonsdale*, lengthened it but chose not to rename it. (Waddingtons)

Left: The converted former tanker *Brocodale H* (see page 74) sunk in the Trent, near Althorpe, in February 1997 with its cargo of Trent aggregate being removed by grab. (John Noble Collection)

Below: Ribblesdale H built at Knottingley in 1950 as a double-skinned tanker for work on the Manchester Ship Canal, was purchased by CBK Construction of Goole after finishing work as a tanker on the Severn waterways. After conversion by them to a dry cargo vessel, it was occasionally used as a workboat and is shown in this capacity, fitted with shear legs, lifting out the old gates of Naburn lock, near York in the late 1970s. (C. Nightingale Collection)

Right: The following four pictures all relate to the same barge which began existence as Whitakers' *Humber Navigator.* The vessel was built by YDDC in 1964 as a dry cargo barge and is seen in Hull harbour between Drypool and North bridges as the river bares out with the ebb and craft sit on the river bed. After lengthening, the barge collected its final cargo of aggregate in mid-1973 and was converted to a tanker (see page 71) shortly after.

Below: Whitakers' *Humber Navigator* was sold in 1989 and renamed *Falmouth Endurance* before moving to the south coast to perform bunkering duties. It is shown in 2001, as a tanker after returning to the Humber, leaving the Trent's Newark Nether Lock whilst making a trial run up the Trent. (Andy Horn)

Falmouth Endurance under conversion back to a specialised dry cargo vessel in the dry dock in Albert Dock, Hull, after acquisition by Robert Wynn & Sons. The ex-dry cargo vessel and ex-tanker was then renamed *Inland Navigator* and used to transport abnormal loads. (Mike Brown)

Robert Wynn & Sons' *Inland Navigator*, formerly *Falmouth Endurance* and *Humber Navigator*, approaching Newark Town Lock assisted by the tug *Micky* in 2004 whilst handling an outsize load on the Trent. (Mike Brown)

Acaster Water Transport's ex-Harker tanker *Easedale* approaching Bulholme lock whilst on the Besthorpe–Whitwood aggregate deliveries, after conversion to a dry cargo vessel in 1968 and lengthening by 36½ft at Waddingtons' yard in 2005 to give it a capacity of 450 tons. The engine was replaced at the same time by a 375hp Kelvin. (Mike Brown)

Whitakers' *Coalite* (see page 15), converted to a mobile steaming unit for cleaning the tanks of other craft, moored alongside *Sirwin* in Hull Harbour and still working for the company in 1979 after nearly seventy years of service.

Other titles published by Tempus

Tugs and Towing Barges on the Humber Waterways

MIKE TAYLOR

Featuring the tugs and towing barges that have moved cargoes on the Humber's inland waterways from early in the twentieth century to the present day, Mike Taylor's descriptions of the relevant traffic movements are accompanied by illustrations from Lincolnshire, Nottinghamshire and Yorkshire.

0 7524 3804 2

Shipping on the Humber The South Bank

MIKE TAYLOR

Mike Taylor has collated a diverse selection of material to illustrate the history of shipping on the river Humber.using a variety of images and maps. and revealing the history of the growth and decline of the industry and the area.

0 7524 2780 6

Shipping on the Humber The North Bank

MIKE TAYLOR

This fascinating collection of images depicts the entire history of shipping on the river Humber. It features many illustrations and maps, accompanied by interesting and informative text.

0 7524 3116 1

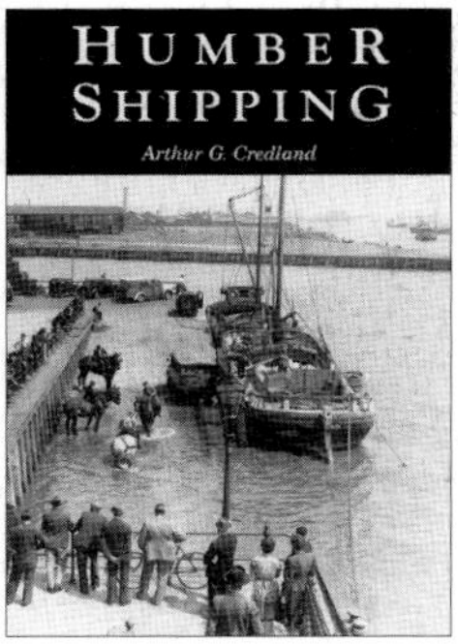

Humber Shipping

ARTHUR G. CREDLAND

Over a long period the city of Kingston upon Hull grew to be one of Britain's major ports and shipbuilding centres. But now many docks and warehouses have gone and the fishing fleet is greatly reduced. Illustrated with over 200 images, Humber Shipping reveals the changing faces of the Humber's maritime history.

0 7524 3085 8

If you are interested in purchasing other books published by Tempus, or in case you have difficulty finding any Tempus books in your local bookshop, you can also place orders directly through our website

www.tempus-publishing.com